love

makes

room

love

makes

room

AND OTHER THINGS I LEARNED
WHEN MY DAUGHTER CAME OUT

staci frenes

Broadleaf Books
Minneapolis

Published in association with Books & Such Literary Management,
52 Mission Circle (Suite 122), PMB 170, Santa Rosa, CA 95409-5370.

"Making Room" song lyrics written by the author and used by
permission. Stone's Throw Music, 2008.

Scripture taken from the Holy Bible, New International Version®, NIV®.
Copyright ©1973, 1978, 1984, 2011 by Biblica, Inc.™ Used
by permission of Zondervan. All rights reserved worldwide.
www.zondervan.com The "NIV" and "New International Version" are
trademarks registered in the United States Patent and Trademark
Office by Biblica, Inc.™

Cover design by Joel Holland

Print ISBN: 978-1-5064-6863-1
eBook ISBN: 978-1-5064-6864-8

For Abby Rae,
who's been showing me what brave looks like
since she entered the world

I'm making room, letting in the light
I'm making room for the wind to dance through
For the music, for the laughter
For the breath of life to happen
It's long overdue
I'm making room
For you

contents

contents

foreword

i wish this book had found me years ago when I was drowning in fear and uncertainty. When I was convinced there was no hope and no one I could turn to for help. It would have changed everything.

I, too, am the mother of a gay child. My son spent his whole life trying to come out to me. Every time he tried, I nipped it in the bud. Changed the subject. I didn't want to have that conversation, and even if I did, I didn't have the vocabulary for it. As a result, our home wasn't a safe space for him. He was forced to "check himself at the door"—he had to look elsewhere for the love and acceptance he needed. When he finally did come out to me, at twenty-one, he was already a grown man. My biggest regret is that I lost his entire adolescence with him.

At the time, I had no idea how to process what our family was going through or where to turn for answers. As an evangelical Christian, the only context I had for "homosexuality" was what I had absorbed in my twenty-plus years attending our neighborhood Southern Baptist church. I knew what my church believed about gay people. So when my son came out, I knew I couldn't go to my church friends or my pastor with my fears and questions. I felt like I had to choose between my faith and my child.

I was clinging to a certain version of faith, and it almost killed me, and it deeply harmed my son.

What I wouldn't have given for this book during those long, sleepless nights I spent worrying about my son. To read the words of a mom like me who comes from a faith background like mine sharing a story much like my own and knowing that the words "love makes room" would have resonated with me. Her story would have reassured me that what I was feeling was normal. Given me a vocabulary for what I was experiencing and, more importantly, the permission to express it. Her story would have offered me hope and shown me a way through—a way that allowed both my son and my faith to flourish.

Staci's story shines light on a path that many parents find hopelessly dark. With raw honesty and authenticity, she invites us to discover, right along with her, how faith and support for our children can start with a fierce devotion to making room—for important conversations; for tough questions, laughter, hope; and ultimately, for a reimagined future.

When I meet and talk with thousands of LGBTQ young people across the country, I'm reminded they all have in common the need to be seen and loved for who they are. But many kids who come out in Christian homes experience just the opposite. As a result, they face higher than normal risks for depression and suicidal ideation.

Parents of faith, we *must* do better at understanding and embracing our LGBTQ children. Their lives (and frankly, ours) are depending on it. It's why I started Free Mom Hugs, a nonprofit foundation dedicated to educating families, churches, and civic leaders and encouraging them to not only affirm the values of the LGBTQ community but celebrate them. And it's why stories like Staci's are so important—because they are the virtual Free Mom Hugs in book form that so many parents, guardians, relatives, friends, and LGBTQ children need: a friend and confidant along the way.

The mom I was back when my son came out desperately needed the honesty, wisdom, and insight that *Love Makes Room* offers. It's the resource I was looking for when I thought no one could possibly understand what I was going through. And it's the guidebook every parent needs on what can sometimes be a scary and confusing but also beautiful journey.

—Sara Cunningham
Founder, Free Mom Hugs

introduction

*S*ome of us go too long, sometimes forever, without telling anyone the painful, difficult parts of our story. We're convinced most people wouldn't understand the dark night we've walked through, and even if they did, we're too ashamed to talk about it in the light. Not long ago the thought of writing a book about an intensely personal struggle that spans several years—and a transformational shift in my faith—would have scared me speechless. I didn't think I'd ever feel brave enough, smart enough, or just plain ready enough to tell it.

It's taken a long time to gain enough perspective to make sense of it myself. The events that happened and the truths they taught me needed time to gestate, mature, and ripen before I could share them publicly. If I had tried to write this book earlier, I'm convinced it would have been bitter fruit, with none of the sweetness or complexity only time and faith can work out.

Nine years ago, when our teenage daughter told us she was gay, my tidy Christian faith began to unravel. In a Jesus-loving, evangelical-churchgoing family, this just didn't seem possible.

What I'd always believed to be the biblical truth regarding homosexuality suddenly didn't fit with my new reality, and trying to reconcile the two felt insurmountable, overwhelming.

Slowly, in the months and years following Abby's coming out, I struggled to make room for my daughter's sexual orientation, entering a process of letting go of my own expectations and dreams for her and accepting and loving the person she was. I wrestled with a faith I'd always leaned on, finding few assurances or guarantees. I learned to live in the tension of uncertainty and to my surprise discovered a richer, truer relationship with my daughter and with God because of it.

I wrote this book to shed some light on an inner journey that for many of us who are rooted in evangelical Christian culture is so tangled with conflicting feelings, opinions, and convictions, it's difficult to see a way through. And I wrote this book to illuminate the ways in which my heart and my faith needed to stretch and grow in order to make room for a bigger understanding of what it meant not only to have a gay daughter but to be a follower of Jesus.

I knew there were others like me who experienced a crisis of faith when their child came out as LGBTQ and who were struggling with how to respond and what to feel, think, or believe. I wanted to be as honest as possible, for their sake, about the process by which I came to accept and understand my daughter as gay in the context of my Christian faith.

In a later chapter in this book (*Love and the Last Word*), I describe how I arrived at my beliefs regarding the Bible and homosexuality. It's near the end for two reasons: First, in writing this book, as in life, it took a long time to recognize the biases and beliefs ingrained in me as a result of my upbringing—a crucial series of steps that led to a better understanding of what I believe now. It seemed fitting to explore that later rather than earlier in the book. Second, I wanted the people and unfolding events of this story to help the reader, as they did me, see that theology is best understood in the context of real life.

Speaking of real people, most of the family and friends who played a part in this story are called by their real names and gave their permission for me to include them in this book. I'm especially grateful for my husband, Abe, and our two kids, Zach and Abby, for allowing me to write about such a private and difficult season in our family life. I tried to honor each of them in the telling of this story. Where I felt it was appropriate, I changed some names and details to protect people's privacy.

We all come to these complex questions about faith, sexuality, and identity from such different backgrounds, it would be impossible for one story to speak for everyone's. I don't assume my process or the conclusions I came to in my own faith will be the same as yours. And the truth is, I'm still learning, still making room for new ways of thinking and talking about this topic.

Even so, I hope you find the insights, life lessons, and wisdom I share in this book valuable and useful. It would be my great joy if you considered this book your companion, wherever you're starting from and wherever you end up. I hope it helps you make room for your own questions, conversations, and a growing understanding of what it means to love God and each other.

1

the dress

MAKING ROOM FOR HOPE
IN THE MIDST OF LOSS

*t*he saying "Into every life a little rain must fall" might have applied to us in the spring of 2010 if the only thing we'd had to contend with was the loss of our home. As it happened, the heavens opened and sent a gale-force hurricane.

It was true: we were moving, again. And I hated moving with a contempt born of familiarity. In our first ten years of marriage, my husband (Abe) and I moved nine times. Between finishing college, moving in with my parents, changing jobs, and needing a bigger place to start a family, we basically had a revolving account with U-Haul.

But this move was a particularly hard one. Now in our forties with two teenagers, after years of schlepping our earthly belongings from place to place, we had finally settled into a house that felt like a real home. It felt like *us*—we'd handpicked everything from the paint colors to the bathroom fixtures. When the housing market plummeted less than two years after we moved in, taking our home's value, all our savings and reserves, and most of Abe's mortgage business down with it, we felt hollowed out in every way: emotionally, physically, and spiritually.

Losing a home is way up there on the list of things that make you want to stay in bed all day. I sank into a depression deeper than I'd ever experienced. Not only was I grieving the huge loss; I was ashamed. Afraid people would think we had mismanaged or been reckless with our money even though logic told me that wasn't the case.

What made it worse was that I was raised with the belief that if you prayed *fervently* and with enough faith, God would answer. I felt duped. I *had* prayed. A lot. I fasted. I even asked my church, family, and friends to pray, too, for a windfall, an eleventh-hour miracle. None came. No divine intervention, no answers. All that was left now was the painful task of packing up our dream house and leaving.

On a hot afternoon during our last week in the house, I walked into the garage to survey the damage left by the movers who came through the day before, taking everything that wasn't attached. A few lonely items littered the concrete floor: an umbrella, a toilet plunger, scattered hangers, a lamp base. Each one had a purpose and a place in my life once, and it seemed odd to see it all randomly strewn about like debris from a picked-over lost and found bin. I felt a stab of desperate nostalgia and was half tempted to start gathering it all up like Steve Martin in *The Jerk*. "All I need is this plunger . . . and this umbrella . . . and maybe these hangers . . ."

Glancing up into the rafters, I saw a slender rectangular box with faded, fancy blue lettering on the side. My wedding dress had been tightly sealed in that box for over twenty years. The movers must have overlooked it. In spite of my sadness, I smiled to see it—a relic from another age, vintage in both years and sentiment. I was just shy of twenty-one years old when I walked down the aisle in that dress—a lifetime ago—but I could still conjure the memories: the sequined bodice as it caught the light, the silky feel of the sheer sleeves. I remember my husband watching me walk toward him in that dress, feeling like a fairy-tale princess for the first time in my life.

I'd seen it on a willowy brunette in one of the hundreds of *Bride* magazines I looked through and immediately knew it was *my* dress. In that pre-internet era, it took several weekends of calling and visiting every bridal shop in Northern California to find it. When we did, it was on sale! A personal best for Mom, the master ninja of bargain hunting. Standing in front of the mirror, I finally understood why movies and TV shows made such a fuss about finding the perfect dress: you can't underestimate the power of a girl's dream to marry her prince in a fairy-tale gown.

At the time, I thought it was a little impractical and expensive to preserve my wedding dress in a hermetically sealed box, but my lack of sentimentality lost out to my mother-in-law's insistence that *one day you'll want to pass this on to your daughter.* Truthfully, I was glad we had saved it. Over the years, I loved knowing it was there for Abby, our youngest and only girl. One day, she would walk down the aisle toward her future husband in the same dress I had worn. It felt like a profound, meaningful connection the two of us could share on the most special day of our lives. The fact that it survived our ten-plus moves unscathed was practically a miracle.

With the passing of time, the dress took on more than merely sentimental value; it came to symbolize the future I imagined for Abby. Like every mom, I wanted my girl to grow up and have a life filled with laughter, purpose, and most of all, love. I wanted her to be someone's dream come true, someone's storybook princess to have and to hold, in sickness and in health, for better or for worse. I imagined that someone to be a good, strong man. The kind of man who would hold her hand in the car, drive to Walgreens in the middle of the night to buy cough medicine when she was sick, provide a good home. The kind of man I married.

Sometimes I allowed myself to imagine more, so much more, about Abby's future. She would have children, and over the years, her family would fill my home with noise and chaos at Thanksgiving and Christmas and as often as I could get them to visit. They would live close enough for spontaneous dinners, grandkid pickups, and afternoon get-togethers at the park. So many carefully chosen dreams, packed like fine china in my imagination, waiting to be unwrapped.

Looking at the dress box again, a realization seized me: I almost forgot for a moment those dreams were now just impossible fantasies. A few weeks earlier, our sixteen-year-old daughter had told me she was gay. I never saw it coming, and to say I wasn't prepared would be a massive understatement. It felt like a sucker punch from the universe or God or Satan—I didn't know where it came from—and it about knocked me out. In the time it took for Abby to spill out her tearful secret one morning on the way to school, I felt what was left of my tidy Christian world crumble to dust and my hopes for her future, and mine, slip through my hands.

In this new reality, there was no room for illusions—those fantasies would only be tormenting me now. I would have to leave them behind, like all the lovingly chosen features of this house we were losing. I sank down on the concrete floor of the garage and felt the tears and questions I had so deliberately avoided rush in like a flood.

This wasn't supposed to happen in a family like ours. My husband and I were people of deep faith, Christ followers, worship leaders. Having a gay daughter fit absolutely nowhere in my framework of family, career, or faith. I was already in the throes of grief and anxiety over losing our house; Abby's unexpected news put me into a kind of emotional coma. I stopped praying. I couldn't allow myself to feel. The personal and spiritual implications were so big, so much to deal with that I just *didn't*—and I was determined to keep it that way until I got through this move. On the surface, I was a body going through the motions—packing moving boxes, cooking dinner, driving Abby to and from school—all as an epic storm raged deep inside me.

Seeing the dress now, I felt the tumultuous waters beneath the surface threatening to rise. And suddenly, God and I were back on speaking terms, apparently, because everything out of my mouth was a desperate question that demanded an answer.

Where would she end up?
What kind of life would she have?
Who would take care of her?
Would she ever have children?
Would God—could God—forgive her?
What would we tell our church?
Why did my friends get to have daughters who would get married and have babies and live normal lives? Why did I have to be the one to have a gay daughter?

I thought about something a well-meaning friend had said when I told him about Abby: "God must have known you were brave enough to handle this. I don't think I could." If he could only see me now. I wasn't "handling" this at all. I wanted to scream, "*I'm not brave! I'm scared to death!*" The implication that having a gay daughter was something God singled me out for because I was braver than someone else infuriated me. In that moment, I would have owned up to being a coward in a heartbeat if it meant I could have my ordinary life—my comfortable guarantees—back.

All my adult life, I had been a Christian, yet in this moment, I had no sense of the peace promised in Scripture, felt no comfort in the Bible verses I'd known since I was a child. I heard no answers from a God I desperately wished would speak to me in the chaos of this storm.

I sobbed until my eyes started to swell shut. Everything inside of me ached to turn back the clock to before Abby told me she was gay, to the familiar, comfortable world I had clung to all these years. To the hope I'd wrapped up so tightly, along with my wedding dress, inside that box. I hated being forced to let go of the assurance of a happy future, a *normal* life with the only daughter I had.

A disorienting loss of certainty overcame me as I tried to imagine what was ahead for her, for us. Trusting in God's goodness and sovereignty had always created a big, open space in my faith when it came to my children. When I thought about their futures, I could always envision happy, blessed lives filled with love and companionship for both of them. Now, though, the terror and unknown of what it meant for Abby to be gay loomed so large and daunting, it blocked my view of any kind of future for her.

The faith I had lived by since childhood and the daughter I loved with my whole being were now at odds in my heart. Overwhelmed with questions, sitting on the cold concrete floor of my garage that day, I didn't know how I could ever find room for both.

Days later when we pulled out of the driveway for the last time toward a future I couldn't yet envision, a nagging worry plagued me: Did we have everything we needed?

Deciding what to throw away and what to save was always the hardest part about moving. With all of the unknowns, all of the room for error in the process of packing, organizing, and sorting through boxes, inevitably a few things got left behind or lost in the shuffle. A perfectly good pair of shoes forgotten in a closet, a favorite coffee mug accidentally thrown in with the Goodwill items. How could I be sure we had checked everywhere, remembered everything? And how could I even know what we would need if we'd never been where we were going?

As many times as I've done it, I still find any move scary, whether it's from one physical place to another or one season of life to another. Some people are cut out for adventure and don't feel the need for road maps, blueprints, or navigation systems. Not me. I like knowing where I'm going and knowing I'll have what I need when I get there. Funny how it rarely works out that way. Someone wise once said the definition of *faith* was balancing the knowing with the unknowing. Leaving our home that day, my heart felt weighed down by all of the unknowing.

In the end, I'm not sure why I brought the dress with us. Maybe force of habit, maybe the sheer tenacity of hope made me pull the box down from the rafters, dust it off, and put it in the car. I thought about leaving it—a vintage treasure for the next homeowner to discover—but at the last minute, I decided to take it.

Some part of me must have known I couldn't hold on to everything it represented any more than I could keep living in a house we no longer owned. My dreams for a perfect home and a "perfect" marriage for Abby were now painful souvenirs from another era, a place and time I could never go back to. Leaving them meant letting go of any illusions of control I had. And yes, they were illusions. I couldn't have predicted a major financial crisis, nor did I have a magic ball showing me Abby's future. But I'd projected what I *wanted* to see for so long that I was convinced the tenacity of my belief could make it a reality.

Bringing the dress into the unknown future we were entering, I knew, was making room for something essential I didn't want to forget or lose. Not so much the ghosts of dreams past but the possibility that there could be new dreams. They had no outline or form yet—and wouldn't for a long time. First, the grief and doubts and questions clamoring for my attention would need to be faced, terrifying as they were. But I wanted to believe, even if I didn't see it yet, that a future existed for Abby. One filled with light and goodness, not overshadowed by my dark fears. And I wanted to believe both God and I would be in that future with her, whatever it would look like.

Setting aside one small corner of my heart for hope, I thought, was at least a start.

2

tears in the rain

MAKING ROOM
FOR THE UNEXPECTED

*a*ny mama who spends a lifetime listening to her girl talk her heart out recognizes what a precious commodity that exchange is. When our daughters come to us with their heartaches and victories, their curiosities and frustrations, their vulnerable and proud moments, and we make room for all of it—acknowledging and validating them—an impenetrable bond is forged between us. We rely on that bond to hold fast when feelings get hurt, egos get ruffled, anger flares. And we trust it to create a safe space for telling the truth, no matter how big or scary it might turn out to be.

Though at the time I wasn't ready to appreciate it, in retrospect, I was grateful for those open lines of communication and bonds of trust allowing Abby to tell me what must have been the most devastating secret she'd ever kept from me. I realize now what a big risk it was for her to tell me she was gay at such a young age, especially having grown up in a conservative Christian family like ours.

Looking back on the months leading up to that conversation, I don't know how I missed seeing she was carrying such a heavy secret and how desperately she needed to share it with me. Regret still haunts me. *I should have seen it; I should have known.* Mom guilt is tenacious, and sometimes, I find myself retracing my steps, looking for clues, signs I missed. There must have been some; I just wasn't putting them all together to form the right conclusion. And for that—for being unable to discern what was wrong and help her—I don't know how to forgive myself.

Years ago, I had a dream about Abby. In it, she was just a toddler, playing outside with the neighbor kids. Through an open window, I could hear she was upset, impatient about something. I knew from the strained, thin stretch of her voice that she was tired, overstimulated. Anyone else listening would have just heard a whiny little girl, but I knew exactly what was wrong. I turned to my husband in the dream and said, "She needs a nap," and that was it. It was so simple and uneventful, but I woke up in tears.

Something about knowing my child's voice so intimately and being able to give her exactly what she needed in that moment—what every mother longs for—made me aware of how frightened and helpless I feel when I don't know what's wrong and I can't help her.

———

Abby Rae entered the world with a big personality and a fiercely strong will, and I seldom had to wonder what she needed because she always let me know—in no uncertain terms. Unlike her quiet, reserved older brother, Zachary, Abby talked a blue streak, mastering full sentences at sixteen months, expressing her thoughts and feelings in a steady stream of words throughout her entire childhood. When she hopped in the car after school, I never had to ask, "How was your day?" because I heard all about it, whether I wanted to or not. Abby told me what was going on in her heart, her head, her body, her classes, her friendships. All of it. I loved that about her—and our relationship.

An old soul, Abby frequently waxed philosophical even as a child. When I put her to bed at night, she loved asking big meaning-of-life questions just before drifting off to sleep. Once when Zachary was attempting to calculate how many presents she'd get for her birthday by the number of friends coming to the party, she'd interrupted him with a dramatic sigh. "Oh, Zach," she said in a world-weary voice, "presents aren't my life; *people* are my life." She was four years old.

Abby's talkative, ebullient personality was a constant in our lives until the beginning of her junior year, when she became inexplicably quiet and reticent. Long bouts of silence replaced her usual "Mom, guess what!" during our after-school car rides home. She would come through the door and head straight up to her room, staying there for hours, reluctant to come down even for dinner, claiming she had too much homework. But her first quarter grades proved otherwise, falling below her usual As and Bs. I assumed typical adolescence was partly to blame, but this felt heavier. Something wasn't right.

One evening in the fall of that same year, I went out to our back patio, following the sound of crying. Since they were infants, I've had supersonic mom radar and could hear my kids crying across distances and through walls. I trusted my instincts and my ears and, sure enough, found Abby on a lounge chair sobbing alone in the chilly darkness. I hugged her tightly for a while, rubbing her back, waiting for the sobs to subside so we could talk it out like we always did. Something was breaking her heart, and if I knew my girl, she would tell me what it was.

But she didn't tell me what was wrong that night or for many more nights during that school year. The dark silence settled in, her grades continued to drop, and her door stayed closed. We got calls from the school informing us that she'd been missing classes. She started smoking. She became secretive about where she was going, who she was with. If we asked her for details, she would get bristly, resentful. When we talked to her about our concerns, she became distant, unconcerned about the consequences of her actions or about breaking the trust between us: normally, both would have upset her deeply.

When I think about the countless hours Abby was alone in her room during those months, how I heard her sobbing through the door, telling me to go away, the guilt almost doubles me over. Surely, I think, a good mother should have broken the door down. A good mother should have demanded that her teenage daughter talk to her about what was going on. Yet I knew from seeing our son struggle through those teen years that as our kids get older and start figuring out life on their own terms, there are some lines we can't cross. Some things we need to let them wrestle with on their own. I had to believe this was one of those times.

Abby would let me into her room and her pain when she was ready.

———

It was raining hard the day she was finally ready to talk. I was irritated that we were running late for school, and neither my daughter's gloominess nor the torrential rain helped lift my mood. We got in the car and drove in tense silence for a couple of minutes. Abby plugged her phone into the car stereo, and Bon Iver's "Skinny Love" began to play. I glanced over and noticed she was crying, her face turned toward the passenger window.

"What's wrong?" I asked, touching her arm.

She pulled away, moving closer to her side. "Nothing."

The sound of rain and Bon Iver's haunting falsetto filled the car.

In the morning, I'll be with you
But it'll be a different kind

The crying was gaining momentum now, her shoulders shaking with it. I reached over and grabbed a napkin from the glove compartment and handed it to her.

"Well, it can't be nothing if you're this upset . . ."

She didn't respond or look away from her window; she just kept sobbing and wiping her nose. We were getting closer to the school.

"Well, I'm not leaving you at school like this. Let's go somewhere and talk."

"I don't want to talk about it."

My mind ran a quick scan of what I knew, which, lately, wasn't much. Had she been in an argument with one of her friends? Was something going on at school—a conflict with a teacher or another student? Was she on her period? I was groping in the dark.

"Abby, honey, this is crazy. Why won't you tell me what's going on with you lately? You've been so sad, and I just want to help. But I can't if you don't let me in."

She looked over at me and practically shouted in frustration, "I can't tell you what's wrong, Mom! If I tell you what's wrong, I'll have to tell you everything!"

Not exactly words a mother wants to hear from her hysterically crying daughter on the way to school. What was "everything"? I tried to process what she meant, and nothing I came up with was good. Red flags waved frantically in my head. I was not going to accept her silence—not this time.

I made a sharp right turn into the golf course parking lot across from the school and pulled into an empty space at the far end, away from the other cars. I turned off the ignition, and the windshield wipers ceased their steady swish-swish across the windshield. No more brushing away the rain, I thought, or the pain. Let it pour.

I turned in my seat to face her and started in with the questions, each one more painful to get out than the last.

"Are you in some kind of danger?"

She shook her head no.

"Has someone tried to hurt you? Or . . . touched you inappropriately?"

"No, Mom."

"Are you in trouble at school?"

Again, she shook her head.

"Are you on drugs?"

"No!"

I took a deep breath and checked off the list of worst-case scenarios. *Thank you, God.* Short-lived relief, as the mother of all questions now seemed the only logical one to ask. I held my breath again.

"Are you pregnant?"

My mind raced with the million ways our lives would change if she said yes. I imagined pacing the floor at three in the morning, trying to get an infant to sleep, pushing a stroller around the neighborhood for the umpteenth time while Abby and her friends checked their Instagram feeds at school. My stomach dropped to my knees.

"No," she said.

Another wave of relief filled me. As long as it wasn't that, I could handle anything.

Still she cried.

I urged as gently as I could. "I need you to help me here. Please, tell me what's wrong, Abby."

Finally, she blurted out, "For starters, I'm heartbroken!" A fresh flood of tears followed her outburst, almost doubling her over.

In spite of her obvious turmoil at this confession, I sat back in my seat and let out a long, pent-up sigh. So that's what this was about. Boy problems. My girl's heart was broken. That I could deal with. That I understood.

"Oh, sweetheart. Oh, I'm so sorry, baby." I waited a minute, then asked quietly, hoping to nudge the details out a little more, "Is it someone you've been seeing for a while?"

She nodded.

"Someone you know from school or somewhere else?"

No response.

"Do I know him?"

Still nothing, just more tears. I don't think I've ever witnessed so many at once. I was grasping at straws, desperate to find the source of her misery. And then—maybe it was a look she gave me, a plea to understand, to follow the train of thought that would lead me to the truth—from some distant place (maybe my mother's intuition?), a word emerged. A word that, even as I acknowledged it inwardly, I could hardly bring myself to say out loud.

"Abby, is this about a *girl*?"

Almost imperceptibly, she nodded.

I made the next leap out of sheer gut instinct.

"Are you trying to tell me you're . . . gay?"

Doubled over, sobbing, she nodded again.

I sat for a minute—or an hour, I don't remember—in stunned silence while this revelation moved through me, the enormity of it unfolding slowly, silently, like a thick fog. The rain pounded on the roof of the car and streamed down every window, as though mocking my earlier bravado: *you said let it pour; now here it comes.*

So this was it. The secret weighing her down for the past several weeks, months—maybe even years? I had no idea. It felt surreal, like I'd suddenly been transported to someone else's life. All of the other scenarios I'd questioned her about, frightening as they were to consider, at least I understood. I knew where to file an unwanted pregnancy, a sexual molestation, and a boyfriend breakup in my brain and in my heart. I'd seen some of my friends go through those situations and could imagine, from their experiences, what it was like.

But this I didn't know how to make room for. The strangeness of it, the unexpectedness. How could this even be possible? And how could I not know it? This was the daughter I had carried in my womb, had watched laugh and eat and brush her teeth every single day of her life. The daughter I had encouraged to talk to me, to tell me anything, and thought I'd heard say everything in her sixteen years: that she had a splinter, a headache, a hard math test coming up, but I had never imagined hearing this.

All of my probing, asking questions, not settling for anything but the whole truth—wasn't this where parenting got uncomfortably real? Like forcing myself to look under their beds for the first time in months, horrified at everything that had been piling up. There was no way to *unsee* this, and now

I had to face it like a loving, responsible adult. I knew some parents who simply chose ignorance sometimes because the truth was either too painful to consider or too difficult to deal with.

If I tell you what's wrong, I'll have to tell you everything.

I could have stopped right there and spared myself the turmoil my heart and stomach were in now. An hour ago, I was blissfully ignorant. If only I had just left her alone. If only I'd been content with less than everything. But that wasn't how we rolled, Abby and me. We learned, by trial and error, it was better to talk it out than to keep it in, no matter how tough the subject.

This was a doozy by anyone's standards, and my daughter had done her part by showing her most vulnerable self to me. Now I had to do mine. I had to somehow make room for this revelation she'd just shared with me, as impossible as that seemed in the moment. Anything less would have violated the code of trust and safety we had worked so hard at over the years. I couldn't leave her hanging now. Surely she was guessing what I was thinking, wondering whether I was still on her side, if I still loved her.

I looked over at my daughter. Her sobbing subsided, her breath now in jagged spurts as her shoulders rose and fell shakily. Shoulders, I realized in that moment, which had been carrying an immeasurable weight. Images in my head began to fit together slowly like a jigsaw puzzle: Abby crying on the back deck under the stars, Abby silent on the car rides home from school, Abby closed up in her room for hours. My red balloon, my ray of sunshine, my talkative little bird, silent for months. I hadn't known why until now.

She finally told me her dark secret, and now it was ours to share. I knew, even before I knew what to do with it, she shouldn't carry it alone. That, more than anything else, was unthinkable to me.

I felt my heart crack open, and now it was my turn to cry—for all of the confusion and loneliness she must have been experiencing. My God, what agony she must have felt trying to decide whether to tell me. My unanswered questions and fears would have to wait until I could sort through them better. For now, at least, I would open my heart to this unexpected revelation and keep it tucked away until I knew what to do with it. I owed her that much.

I realized I hadn't said anything since her almost imperceptible nod revealing her secret. I reached across the armrest, across the gulf of pain and silence growing between us, across the chasm of my own confusion and fear of what was ahead, and pulled my girl into the tightest hug I could manage in that cramped space. I whispered in her ear the words I'd been saying to her since she was a little girl: "I love you. We'll get through this together."

3

pacing the floors

MAKING ROOM FOR QUESTIONS

*d*uring those first few weeks after Abby came out to us, life became a new and unfamiliar frontier for our family. We experienced the shock of it in waves, separately and together. Sometimes we tried to talk about it, to find words for the tender, confused feelings and questions, but conversations felt charged and fragile, like stepping around landmines, as we wrestled with our private thoughts. Our normally chatty dinner hours were tight with unspoken tension and forced politeness—we tiptoed around the giant elephant no one knew how to talk about.

The burning question first consuming me: How did this happen? *What caused Abby to be gay?* I had no context for understanding it, and a Google search proved there were about as many possibilities as stars in the sky.

One theory that grabbed me by the heart right away—maybe because I was looking for my part in the equation?—suggested that absent mothers were a factor in a person being gay. For a devastating couple of days, I went down that rabbit hole. However unknowingly, I must have messed something up in her childhood, withheld some essential component of nurturing that caused her to change trajectories and head down the wrong track. I *had* traveled a lot when she was a little girl, was often preoccupied with my work. Surely, I'd been neglectful, and this was the result.

But *was* this my fault? How could I be sure?

I racked my brain and continued searching the web for something that made sense, but in my distressed emotional state, I was neither thorough nor clearheaded. I grasped at straws. When I read somewhere that childhood trauma could be a factor in a person's sexual orientation, I obsessed over that theory for days. Had she been sexually abused? Not that I knew of, but was it possible something happened when she was younger that she never told me about? The tormenting thought haunted me, circling my brain like a vulture.

I also considered that she had been brainwashed by someone or by an experience into believing she was gay. Maybe she experimented sexually with a girl and confused the temporary excitement of that with being gay. If so, it would fade with the infatuation. Besides, there had been a couple of boys she liked since middle school; didn't that prove she *wasn't* gay?

Weeks passed, and none of my initial theories bore out. My daughter didn't seem confused or traumatized, nor did she cease being attracted to girls. This wasn't going away, and apparently, there weren't any simple formulas or answers as to why she was gay.

Neither my own attempts to understand it nor my initial internet research provided a concrete explanation to put my mind and heart at ease. It seemed even the best theologians, psychiatrists, and scientists studying this subject for decades couldn't conclusively say why a person was gay. How could I expect to fully understand it?

I imagined the millions of parents who, for their own reasons, lived every day with unanswered *whys* about their child. Parents who lost sleep regularly like I did, staring bleary-eyed at a page of Google results, looking for that one needle-in-a-haystack article that would finally bring relief, closure. Like me, I'm sure they felt an unreasonable stubbornness, an inability to accept *I'm not sure* as an option because the stakes were too high. We feel responsible for this precious human after all. Shouldn't we know everything there is to know about them?

Making room for all of the questions about why and how my daughter could be gay and what that meant for her spiritual and emotional future wasn't a decision I made once and never had to revisit again. It was a daily, sometimes hourly, struggle to loosen my grip on the need for certainty. A humbling and vulnerable admission of my own limited understanding.

During those first weeks as I battled with my questions, my girl felt lost to me, as though she'd fallen down a deep well. I could see her, but I didn't know how to reach her. Language had always come easily to me, but for a time, it failed me. What words could I possibly use to tell my child that when looking at her, I saw someone I didn't understand? That my heart, my faith, my whole world had been hurled into chaos since learning she was gay? There weren't any words. Even if there were, I knew I could never say them to her.

It didn't help that our family was experiencing growing, or shrinking, pains at the time. After our recent difficult move, our older son, Zach, spread his young adult wings, moved in with friends, and was taking college classes and pursuing musical opportunities in Los Angeles. I missed his even-tempered, unflappable personality; it balanced out his sister's more dramatic temperament. True to character, he took the news of her coming out with hardly a raised eyebrow. I wondered if she shared it with him before telling us, one of those secrets that siblings promise to keep from their parents. Even so, it surprised me when he showed none of the angst or worry his dad and I were experiencing.

With his leaving home, it was now Abby, Abe, and me occupying what felt like three separate worlds under one roof. Each of us navigating in our own way the tough transitions of a move, Zach's absence, and Abby's newly out status.

Many days when Abby was at school and Abe was at work, all I could manage to do was stare out my bedroom window for most of the day, feeling lost. Sometimes I found solace in songwriting, pouring into my lyrics and melodies what I couldn't find words for in real life. It was from that season of deep searching and grief that I wrote the songs for *Everything You Love Comes Alive* and a book on creativity, *Flourish*. I've never been more grateful to create work that felt beautiful and nourishing in a complicated time.

As the spouse of a songwriter, Abe says that for every song I write about something we've gone through together, there's an unwritten one from his point of view. It's a running joke between us,

another in a long list of ways we're about as opposite as two people can get. In music, he listens to
the bass lines, and I listen to lyrics—which is about
all you need to know to have us figured out. He was
right about our having vastly different perspectives
on just about everything, including our daughter
telling us she was gay.

Though he wasn't there for the initial tear-
filled conversation in the car, I told him later on
the phone. The call consisted of mostly silence and
sighing on his end. My normally verbose husband
was at a complete loss for words, ending the conversation with a soft, resigned "Okay. I'll be home
soon." But we didn't talk much about it that day or
for many days after that. It was too big, too daunting to try to put words to it. Only later, when we
started finding the words to convey what we were
each feeling, did I get a glimpse of what was going
on inside of Abe's heart.

What I saw on the outside was avoidance. After
coming home from work that first day to find Abby,
shell-shocked and numb, he held her tightly and
sobbed for a few overwhelming moments, then
told her, "I love you so much, sweetie." After that, he
seemed to withdraw into his own troubled world.
He found reasons to be at work longer than usual,

and when he was home, he could hardly look her in the eye. If they happened to be in the same room, he got uncomfortably quiet.

It was painful to witness. These were my jokesters, my two peas in a pod who could *always* find something to laugh about together. Abby read the signals and, in response, pulled away from her dad. It would take months—years, even—before the sweetness and closeness of their relationship were restored.

One notion Abe and I shared when Abby first came out to us was *this too shall pass*. After all, by the tender age of sixteen, she had experimented with several identities: skater, rocker, hippie, actress. This girl excelled in self-expression and reinvention. Couldn't this be something she was simply trying out, too, like the various hair colors she changed every few months?

I clung to that possibility hard for a while as an explanation that would make all the confusion and questions go away. That kind of thinking could be a dangerous drug though. Sometimes I needed just a small hit of it—a fleeting hope that things could be normal again—to get me through the day. But the drug gradually stopped working; it only made the reality harder to face.

Abe didn't allow himself to hang on as long as I did to the notion that Abby's "gayness" was just a phase. A realist, he faced things head-on and, for the most part, experienced her coming out like a punch to the gut.

To him, it felt like Abby had given him the message that she didn't value men—and by extension, him. When she said, "*I like girls,*" he heard, "*I don't like men.*" He felt she was erasing him from her past, her present, and her future. It devastated him. It was a wound he wasn't able to articulate fully to Abby or even himself for a long while. With time, it became obvious in big and small ways how much Abby loved and needed her dad. Each time she reached out for help, for advice—even for money—the wound inside of him healed a little more. Like most dads, he needed to know he was needed and still an essential part of his daughter's life.

Stronger than my addiction to magical thinking and Abe's feeling of personal rejection was the apprehension filling us—and on bad days, sheer terror—about the spiritual implications of Abby being gay. Our faith background had only one word for it: *sin*. This was no small thing to reconcile. Both of us came to faith in the Assembly of

God denomination, and Abe came from a tradition that had an even longer list of nos that defined his childhood. No movies, no card playing, no listening to or playing rock music, no smoking, no drinking, and no dancing, to name a few.

The message was implicit: do the right thing—do what your church and parents taught you—and good things will happen. And Abe took it to heart. He was a model kid in every way: from good grades in school to class president and überachiever. By nineteen, he had a full-time job managing a health food warehouse, had graduated with honors, and was supporting himself (and me, once we were married) through college. He's always been a does-what-he-says kind of guy. Loyalty and integrity are the pillars of his character.

When Abe found himself in the impossible position of having to pit what he was taught and, to this point always, believed about homosexuality against what he knew about his own daughter, it just about broke him. How could both things be true—that Abby was gay and that the Bible called it a sin? To accept her being "out" would not only go against his religious conscience; it would condemn her to a life without God's forgiveness or mercy.

The unthinkable conflict knocked around violently inside his heart. It tormented his thoughts, upset his stomach, disrupted his entire life.

While I'm an overthinker and a stewer, Abe is a doer. If there's a problem that needs fixing, he goes, undaunted, into action mode. Usually, it involves a roll of duct tape. If the dishwasher is leaking, he'll take it apart and tinker with it until he finds the problem. If there's a trail of ants in the bathroom, he'll figure out the source and set the bait, and the ants disappear by morning. When our kids were younger, he pulled out their splinters, repaired their punctured bike tires, replaced the batteries in their toys, and put just about any broken thing back together. We call him MacGyver or Jerry Rig—there doesn't seem to be anything he can't fix.

When he can't figure something out, he has a habit of pacing the floor, as though walking the same path repeatedly will make the answer materialize. Pacing is also usually how he prays *fervently*—with his whole body because it makes him feel like he's at least doing something to help the situation along.

In my twenties, I had health problems that sometimes landed me in the ER all night. Lying in the hospital bed, it was Abe's prayerful pacing I remember as much as the pain. As a baby, Zach had awful colic, and the only thing that settled him down was Abe holding him in a football hold while he paced for hours. When they were teenagers, if our kids tried to sneak into the house past curfew, it was their dad they came face-to-face with at the door, fresh from pacing—I'd be sound asleep. Pacing has always been Abe's thinking strategy, prayer routine, and therapy all rolled into one.

One evening after dinner, deep into this season of unrest, Abe and I were alone at the dinner table with our questions, our troubled thoughts.

I was beginning to consider that Abby being gay wasn't a flippant choice she had made or a phase she was going through but something deeper and more complicated. I had been reading and meditating on Psalm 139, and I believed that the God who had formed her in my "innermost being" must understand the complexity of her situation in a way I didn't yet. It was a new way of thinking about it, a way that gave me a sense of peace I hadn't felt in weeks.

I wasn't sure what Abe would think about my newfound peace, but I desperately wanted us to come to a meeting of the minds about our daughter. If he could make room for even a tiny glimpse of hope in the midst of his turmoil and questions, the way I was starting to, maybe a small measure of peace would follow for him too. This was a fragile, difficult territory to talk through, but I wanted to try.

"I've been thinking," I said. "Maybe it's going to be okay after all. With Abby. You know?"

"What do you mean, 'okay'? There's nothing about this that's okay."

"I mean, what if God is bigger than all of our questions about this? What if we could trust that God's got Abby and not worry so much about trying to understand it?"

"That would be a nice thought." His tone was dismissive.

"Do you believe it?"

"I believe God loves her. But I also believe the Bible is truth, God's word, and we can't just ignore the verses we don't like. I can't make up my own rules, Stace. Neither can you, and neither can Abby. It is what it is."

"So you're saying if Abby's really gay, you believe she's—what—literally going to hell?" I raised my voice at the end, alarmed at the sound of the words.

"I don't know!" he snapped back, more in desperation than anger.

"You need to stop thinking that way. She's our flesh and blood. Nothing about her has changed, but you've been walking around here like a robot and can barely look at her!"

"How can you say nothing's changed? *Everything* has changed! For one thing, I now know she doesn't want a man in her life—ever! How do you think that makes me feel?"

I didn't have a response to that. I knew he'd have to work that one out on his own.

He continued. "I can't just throw out everything I've believed. That would be like admitting I've been living a lie, following a God I don't even obey."

That riled me up. I was wrestling with some of the same doubts, and I hated how it made me feel—trapped into making an impossible choice.

I said to him, as much as to myself, "How could we possibly obey a God who, it turns out, pulled a prank on us by giving us a daughter who's gay? Something which, by the way, God hates and can't forgive. Because that's what you're saying!" I knew I sounded hysterical, but I couldn't help myself. If he could voice his worst fears, then so could I.

"I don't understand it either, Stace! I just know we can't conveniently pick and choose Bible verses to fit what we want to believe. Do you think this is easy for me?"

I got up from the table and walked toward the stairs that led up to our bedroom. I couldn't stand to hear any more. I was furious at God for putting us in this predicament, and since God wasn't visible at the moment, I turned my anger on Abe.

"Okay," I snapped, "but I'm choosing to believe that when it's all over, we're going to be surprised at all the people *not* going to hell! Including our daughter!" I stomped up the stairs in tears.

I waited for him to come to bed later that night, but he didn't.

Early the next morning, I quickly threw on my robe and headed quietly downstairs to make coffee. Nearing the bottom of the stairs, I could see him pacing the living room floor like a crazed, weary dog. He was searching—prayerfully racking his brain, the heavens—for answers in those paces.

"Have you been up all night?" He stopped pacing and nodded in my direction, bleary-eyed. "Sit. I'll make coffee."

He didn't sit. He stood where he was and said, matter-of-factly, "I came to a conclusion last night."

My heart dropped to my stomach. His tone indicated he meant business. I didn't know what answer he had found in the dark hours of the night, but I wasn't sure I wanted to hear it.

Shaken but resolute, he said, "I don't have any control over the next life, and maybe that's not for me to try and figure out. But as long as she's my daughter, she'll never be loved by anyone outside this house more than she's loved by me."

I don't know what I was expecting him to say—not by a long shot—but I knew it was the exact right thing. I knew this had cost him a long night of wrestling with his soul. A night of surrendering his will and making room for the hardest questions he'd ever asked himself or God. I also knew he was a man of his word. He would put aside whatever issues he still had about Abby being gay and love her with his whole heart. "Fixing" her wasn't an option, he had concluded; loving her was the only right and good thing.

I couldn't have felt more proud of his decision and humbled by his sacrifice in the same moment.

God showed up that night after all. My husband wore the carpet bare with his pacing and his praying, and an answer materialized after a wrestling match of biblical proportions. Like Jacob in the Old

Testament, my husband wrestled with God and received a blessing, but it had a price as steep as Jacob's limp. Abe had to give up the certainty he had carried in his heart since he was a little boy sitting in the pews of his parents' church. The certainty that following the rules would mean your life would turn out the way you wanted it to. The certainty that if you were a Christian, your prayers would be answered and blessings would follow. He surrendered his religion on the altar, exchanging it for unconditional love.

Maybe the resolution Abe found pacing the floors that night wasn't a promise about Abby's eternal soul or a release from the situation. Maybe it was simply the reassurance of God's presence, keeping pace with his own anxious steps. And where God's presence was, he discovered, there was only love. Love quieting his incessant questions. Love bearing the weight of his feelings of rejection. Love giving him the will and the strength to do what the situation—and his daughter—needed most.

Both of us felt overwhelmed and unequipped for the road ahead of us. We had much to learn, demons to face down, unresolved conflicts to work out. But after his long night of the soul, Abe emerged with a clear set of marching orders: he didn't have to have it all figured out; he just had to love his daughter more than anyone else ever would.

And that, we both knew, he could do.

4

sleepovers and crushes

MAKING ROOM FOR AWKWARD CONVERSATIONS

*t*hat old line we parents sometimes use about wishing our kids came with an owner's manual took on fresh meaning after Abby came out to us. What did I know about bringing up a gay teenager? Exactly nothing. Life would have been much easier if I just had some instructions to follow, a guidebook telling me how to avoid the pitfalls, the heartache. But like other times when the answers were anything but clear, the only way through this new landscape was one tentative, sometimes awkward, step at a time.

While I silently navigated a sea of questions and concerns inside my heart, on the surface, I found myself either walking on eggshells, afraid I was going to hurt Abby's feelings if I said something wrong, or worse, burying my head in the sand, withdrawing from her altogether. Neither of these modes of operation made for good parenting. Abby was a teenager, and as far as I knew, teenagers still needed raising. I was going to have to pull myself up by the parental bootstraps and get on with the business of being a mom, whatever that looked like.

If you have a daughter (or niece or grand-daughter), you know there are some fixtures that just come with the girl territory: hormones, crushes, bras, periods, tears, drama, and, of course, sleepovers. Throughout time, girls have packed their cartoon character suitcases with all of their worldly possessions and traveled down the block or across town to spend the night at their best friend's house. It's a shared ritual I participated in as a kid, and I accepted it as normal with my own daughter. However, it was the question of what to do about sleepovers once Abby came out that eventually forced me back into active mom duty.

Abby was an especially social kid, and sleepovers were a regular part of her life, from elementary school all the way through high school. Most Fridays I could almost predict to the minute when she would pop the inevitable question, "Can so-and-so spend the night?" I rarely said no. I loved hearing the girls giggling, shouting over their music, sneaking down the stairs to make popcorn past bedtime. I usually didn't worry about what she and her friends did behind closed doors; my philosophy was unless something was on fire or someone was bleeding, they could manage on their own.

But after Abby came out, certain questions started nagging at me: How did I know which of her friends was more than just a friend? Had I let a girl my daughter was attracted to—maybe even someone she considered a *girlfriend*—spend the night under the guise of an innocent sleepover? Had I unknowingly looked the other way while my daughter experimented with sex—in my own home—at an inappropriately young age? The thought horrified me. Hip as I considered myself, superliberal Mom was definitely *not* my MO.

When it comes to sex, my own upbringing leaned more conservative than most. My parents were churchgoing Christians who taught us that sexual intimacy was only to be shared in the context of marriage. Our faith tradition taught that a girl should "save herself" for her husband and that the Bible clearly discouraged promiscuity outside of marriage. Purity and abstinence were the mantras of my Christian youth group circles.

A popular Christian conference I attended as a teenager called Basic Youth Conflicts outlined in three-ring binder form strict guidelines for courtship and discouraged dating entirely. I knew of a couple of girls in my private Christian high school who were sexually active, but fear of unwanted pregnancy and the belief that premarital sex would put me on the outs with God were enough to convince me to maintain my virginity until I was twenty, when I walked down the aisle with my husband-to-be.

Since Abe came from a similar background and shared my views about sex before marriage, we talked with our kids about it the best way we knew how and then hoped and prayed they would make good choices. We also thought it wise to put some parameters in place that would encourage those good choices, which naturally made us extremely popular with our kids. They let us know regularly we were the *only* parents who didn't allow their friends over when we weren't home. We were the *only* parents who insisted on meeting the parents before we allowed them to stay overnight at a friend's house. We were the *only* parents who had an early curfew. They were prisoners of our old-fashioned morals, apparently, and we were cold, heartless wardens.

You might wonder if we caved under the weight of this disapproval. We did not. Abe and I often shook our heads incredulously at the things those infamous *other* parents allegedly let their kids do. Because we'd both grown up with such clear boundaries and, for the most part, saw the value in them, we felt strongly about drawing lines in the sand with our own kids no matter how much they resisted.

One rule we implemented when our kids hit puberty was if you had someone of the opposite sex in your room, the door stays open. We figured the fear of Mom or Dad walking in would keep things PG at least. What they did elsewhere, of course, was as unknowable to us as a black hole, but in our home, we reserved the right to have a visual on our kids' dating lives at all times.

But after Abby came out to us, those parameters weren't as clear anymore. I was conflicted about how to approach the closed-door rule—never mind the whole sleepover topic. It suddenly got complicated now when her friends came over. How did I know what *kind* of friend this girl was? Should I demand that her door stay open anytime she had a female friend over? That didn't seem fair, since it gave her no privacy. But I wasn't comfortable with it being closed all the time, either, for the same reason I wouldn't be if her brother had a girl in his room at her age. I believed boundaries were a good idea for any teenager with hormones—gay or straight—but I wasn't always sure how to draw them in Abby's case.

Parenting dilemmas I couldn't have anticipated in a million years began to surface in this new landscape. Abe and I joked that we may not understand Abby's attraction to girls, but at least she wouldn't get pregnant if she spent the night with one. We laughed, but it felt strange and counterintuitive to my understanding. I barely gave her male friends a passing glance when they went into her room and shut the door. Wasn't I being a reckless, negligent mother, allowing her to be alone with a boy? But if she wasn't attracted to boys, I figured chances were slim they'd get into any kind of sexual behavior.

The question of sleepovers would require conversations I was sure would be awkward and embarrassing for both of us but that I saw as a necessary evil of parenting. Like checking her homework or making sure she ate her vegetables—no one wants that job, but who else was going to do it?

While I hadn't yet wrapped my mind around all of the emotional, much less spiritual, implications of my daughter being gay, I was still committed to raising a responsible, trustworthy young woman, and with that as my criteria, I could try to determine the best course of action. In this case, that meant making room for a few uncomfortable, squirmy conversations.

They came soon enough. When Abby texted from school one Friday afternoon to ask if a friend could come over to study, our exchange went from simple to complicated in a hot minute.

"Vanessa and I have a huge project due on Monday, so we want to work on it together."

"Oh, okay. I don't think I remember Vanessa . . ."

"She's in my English class; I know I've told you about her."

"Hmmm. Well, okay. Will she be staying for dinner?"

"Yeah, probably."

"I'll make sure there's plenty of food."

"Also, the project will take a while, so is it okay if she spends the night so we can keep working on it in the morning?"

"I don't know, honey."

"Why?"

"Well, I don't really know her."

"But I told you, she's in my English class."

"I know, but . . . I don't know what she is to *you*."

"What do you mean?"

"Is she a friend, or is she someone you like another way?"

"Mom, please."

"I'm asking because it makes a difference."

"She's just a *friend*!"

"Are you sure?"

"Yes!"

I needed more information. I tried to probe delicately.

"But is she someone you're attracted to? Like, okay, she's just a friend now, but could it possibly . . . develop into something else?"

She laughed. "Mom, you're way overthinking this!"

Of course I'm overthinking this! I wanted to snap back at her. I couldn't remember a single situation in my history as a mom where my parental skills had been tested at this kind of graduate level. If someone had told me that one day I'd be having *this* conversation with my daughter, I would have looked at them cross-eyed with disbelief and laughed too.

Only I wasn't laughing now.

"Abby, I'm just trying to understand. Because if this girl is someone you're attracted to, then the answer is no, she can't spend the night."

"Mom, you're being ridiculous. I have *friends* who are girls!"

I was frustrated now. "Well, how am I supposed to be able to tell the difference? They all look the same to me!"

She was quiet for a second, then said, "You'll just have to trust me."

She had a point. A lot of this would come down to trust. I hated the thought of having to interrogate her like this every time she wanted to have someone spend the night, but I also believed in mother's intuition, and she was a teenager, *and* this was all new to me. Trusting her wasn't as simple as it sounded.

For a few months, we waded through sets of those dreaded Q&As, both of us cringing every time. Maybe it surprised us both that, for the most part, we made some progress. I grew to trust her a little more, and she grew to tolerate, if not wholeheartedly embrace, my need to keep the boundaries clear.

When she did have friends over, I'd find reasons to nonchalantly walk past her room and check on them. I wasn't above peeking into rooms, listening in on conversations, glancing over shoulders at texts—all the classic sneaky mom moves came in handy more times than she'll ever know. If Abby happened to catch me, she'd roll her eyes—the universal sign for *you're being so lame*—but I didn't care. I was undaunted, determined to excel at being lame if it meant keeping my girl honest. And she was, for the most part.

Until she fell in love with one of her best friends and it got messy.

I don't think Abby planned to fall in love. It was a slow progression that moved at a natural pace. They had met and bonded sharing a class at school together, and before long, studying and doing homework together turned into doing most everything together.

Valerie became a regular fixture in our home, and in the beginning, their friendship felt like a much-needed breath of fresh air for all of us. I adored her and was delighted the two of them had become such good friends. She brought out the light, silly side of Abby, and it made me happy to see *her* happy. In every way, the friendship felt so innocent, so *normal*, that I was lulled into believing it would stay that way forever.

I might have seen glimpses of it—how close they sat together on the couch, the shrieks of laughter as they wrestled around in Abby's room, long notes to each other I discovered when I was cleaning—but much of it seemed so typical of girls' friendships that I didn't connect the dots until Abby started giving me hints that their relationship had changed. Exactly what that entailed I wasn't sure, but before I had time to process it, the two of them had become more than just BFFs.

My heart deflated at this turn of events. Suddenly, my mom radar had to kick into high gear, on the lookout for foul play and enforcing rules that didn't apply before. The bedroom door had to stay open. No overnight stays or long periods in the house if we weren't home.

I'm sure Abby resented these restrictions interfering with the comfortable familiarity of their relationship. And I hated it too—but for different reasons. Life felt almost normal for a while, as it did before Abby came out, and I allowed myself to hope that maybe . . . just maybe . . . it really was just a stage. This was a reminder that it wasn't and probably never would be. I wanted their relationship to go back to the idyllic, platonic friendship I knew and understood, where *girlfriend* meant only one thing.

This new dimension to their relationship also stirred up a heavy question in my heart: How did the Bible—and more importantly, God—view this? Up to this point, my prayers about Abby were mostly cries for understanding. Why was she was attracted to girls? How did her sexual orientation—if that's truly what this was and not a phase like I'd first assumed—fit with my belief that she was made "in the image of God"? I was beginning to trust that God knew and loved her on a level even I couldn't yet understand, and it gave me an indescribable sense of relief and comfort.

With this new development, though, I wasn't sure how to pray. I didn't see anything inherently "sinful" in Abby being attracted to Valerie; it evolved so gradually from friendship, I found it hard to know at what point it needed addressing as wrong. Should I pray for the feelings to go away? And if they didn't, should I forbid them to see each other? Neither seemed like a reasonable option. The best approach seemed to be enforcing the house rules we'd always felt were appropriate for our kids. At the very least, they would minimize the amount of time they had alone and thus limit opportunities for intimate physical contact. Rules I hoped would serve as guardrails, caution signs, to keep them from careening into emotional territory they weren't prepared for.

In spite of my conflicted feelings about it, I couldn't have asked for a sweeter experience of witnessing my daughter fall in love for the first time. It was a gift to see their relationship begin innocently and truly heartwarming to watch it blossom over time. Even my husband admitted that the fear that had been gripping our hearts since Abby came out began to melt when seeing the two of them together.

Valerie felt like a second daughter in our home, and her transition from friend to girlfriend didn't change how dear she was to us. We caught a little glimpse of what life could be like in this new world and thought if our daughter could find someone who made her this happy for the rest of her life, maybe we could learn to accept it. That realization was an unexpected surprise.

When I first learned Abby was involved with a girl, the one she'd told me about when she came out to me, I didn't even want to know her name. As I saw it, Abby was the victim and "that girl" seduced and brainwashed her into thinking she was gay. I made all kinds of not-so-generous assumptions about her without ever meeting her: she was trouble, she was immoral, she was taking advantage of my daughter. At the time, it was the only explanation I wanted to accept for Abby's unexpected coming out.

Later, when I had the opportunity to get to know Alex in the years she and Abby remained friends, I saw that none of those things I had believed about her was true. It took just one conversation to discover she was smart, kind, and funny. Like my own daughter, Alex had a family that loved her and wanted to understand and support her in coming out to them. I felt ashamed at how harshly I'd viewed her, how easy it was to make her the villain in the story I told myself about Abby rather than face the truth.

Now as I thought about Abby and Valerie and the natural way their relationship blossomed and grew, it made my heart ache to think someone might characterize Abby in the same way I did Alex; Alex had been the scapegoat for my fears, bias, and ignorance at the time—all because I didn't take the time to get to know her.

There would inevitably be people who looked at Abby that way, who saw *only* her sexual identity—not her tender heart, her courage, her sense of humor, or any of the other wonderful attributes I see. The same way I knew there were some people who only saw skin color and never the human being when they looked at a Black person. To get to know anyone, especially someone who's different from us, I was learning, you have to make room for simple, if sometimes awkward, conversations. They proved to be the best antidote I knew for the toxic ways fear sometimes made us behave toward each other.

In the few months since Abby had come out, I already felt my heart expanding in ways I didn't know it could. I'd known my daughter all her life, yet I was discovering in this new season of life—hers and mine—there were things about her I still needed to learn. Neither of my kids came with specific instructions; each required a level of discernment, insight, and wisdom no manual could prepare me for. In Abby's case, the operating instructions were so unfamiliar and new, the only way to not be overwhelmed by it all was to keep asking questions, keep listening, and keep my heart open for all of the things I still needed to learn.

5

whose story is this?

MAKING ROOM FOR PERSPECTIVES

*m*oments and milestones in Abby's senior year of high school flew by quickly, like scenes in one of those indie art films you don't understand until after it's all over, if you ever do. I wanted to push pause several times that year in order to process what was happening—cry, pray, journal, write a song, assume the fetal position, whatever it took—before moving on like the well-adjusted parent I wanted to be. I was lucky if I could catch my breath.

One big adjustment involved coming to terms with Abby being out in the public spaces where she was starting to become more open about being gay, like at school and on social media. I was only talking with immediate family and a small handful of close friends about it. I didn't feel safe sharing it with anyone outside of my inner circle. Trying to work through the implications for Abby's future, our family, and even more daunting—my faith—was something I wanted to do *privately*, not in public.

Though I'm comfortable in front of large groups—the result of performing on stages for over half of my life—I'm mostly an introvert. Part of me feels the need to be seen and heard through the songs I write, but it's a rehearsed candor, a guarded vulnerability. There's another side to me that's intensely private, much more comfortable under the radar than in the limelight. I'm constantly conflicted about how much of my personal life to put out there in public. On social media, I usually erred on the side of caution and kept quiet about anything sensitive. Abby's coming out soared way off my sensitivity chart, and it was the last thing I wanted to discuss in public.

In that way, my daughter and I couldn't have been more different. Abby, who entered the world imbued with an extra helping of moxie, was never one to avoid taking risks or rocking boats, and she had no problem being the center of attention. Even as a little girl she moved through the world with a passion and intensity of purpose that said *watch me*. Her self-confidence seemed to come from an unwavering belief that whatever she was doing at the moment—whether she had figured it out yet or not—was worth sharing with the world.

Like most '90s-era parents, we had piles of videotapes showing our kids' milestones: birthday parties, Easter egg hunts, Christmas mornings, and every sweet, tender, or funny moment in between.

All of it captured with a Channel 2 News–size camera on one shoulder. One particular videotape labeled "Abby" was filled with footage of just her, and as a toddler, she constantly and obsessively begged us to watch "The Abby Movie," as she called it. She would sit for hours hitting rewind and playing it over and over, mesmerized by the sight of herself on the TV screen, reveling in being the star of her own show.

At twelve, with just a couple of guitar lessons under her belt, Abby decided to perform a song for our family on Christmas Eve. Insisting we dim the lights and give her our undivided attention, she struggled through a rough rendition of "Silent Night"; the birth of Jesus had some competition that year if my daughter had anything to say about it.

Now as her senior year unfolded, Abby shed the heaviness of her junior year like a butterfly emerging from a chrysalis. She'd always been interested in music, playing in a band since she was in the eighth grade, but she launched out into drama and musical theater with gusto, landing lead roles in both productions she auditioned for, and even joined a small choral ensemble that performed around the area.

As she spread her creative wings, no holds barred, with none of the fragile trepidation I was feeling at the time, I wondered if people knew our secret and what they thought about it. So determined to keep quiet about what was going on in our home, I almost forgot this girl of mine rarely let other people's opinions deter her from living her life out loud. In that regard, I felt proud of her but also anxious that her being openly gay wouldn't always be met with understanding and acceptance.

In the spring, my fear got put to the test when Abby decided to ask a girl to the senior prom. If the idea of prom sends butterflies of excitement fluttering in the hearts of high school girls, for their moms, it can feel like the heavy flapping of dread, what with all of the unwanted extras it brings: extra drama, extra credit card swipes, and a long night of extra anxious hand-wringing. For me, it was all of this and more: I dreaded the extra attention it might bring on Abby and, by extension, me.

I wasn't so much surprised that Abby had met someone new—like most young love, Abby and Valerie's relationship faded out after Valerie moved away in the fall—but asking this new girl to the prom seemed so conventional, so normal, and so *public*. I didn't yet know the particulars, but if I knew my daughter, it wasn't going to play out like

a quiet scene between two wallflowers. Announce-
ments would be made. Pictures would be taken.
Social media would be involved.

My heart recoiled at the thought of the gossip,
comments, and stares she might endure from other
kids and even teachers. Granted, it had been a long
time since I was in high school, and kids Abby's age
were more accepting of same-sex couples, but ours
was a small town; surely not everyone would be on
board with it. I envisioned a *Carrie*-like scene in which
the two of them would be humiliated, laughed at,
made fun of, in front of the entire student body.

Even more insidious was my fear that people
in our small-town community would know our
daughter was gay before *I* was ready for them to
know. We had lived and gone to church there since
our kids were babies. While I was by no stretch
famous, I had sung at most of the conservative
evangelical churches in the area, including my
own, and performed at several citywide events. I
couldn't go to the post office or grocery store without someone telling me they'd seen me sing somewhere. It never bothered me before, but once Abby
came out, the thought of someone from church
asking about her at the grocery store made me
almost break out in hives.

Nevertheless, Abby's plan to ask her date to the prom had a dramatic flair that not only invited attention; it drew a crowd and became the talk of the school for several days. Apparently, just before the last bell of the day, Abby had stood in the hall outside her date-to-be's classroom, guitar in hand and a bouquet of flowers at her feet, singing the song she wrote for the occasion. The sound echoed through the corridor, sending students spilling out of their classrooms, curious to investigate. While a circle of onlookers and friends pressed in, Abby got to the final chorus of the "promposal" just as her date walked out of her classroom. Taking in the song, the flowers, and Abby's expectant grin, she bolted for Abby, and the two of them locked in a tight hug while the crowd clapped and cheered. That's right, *clapped and cheered* like a scene from a Hollywood rom-com.

By the time I heard the story unfold from her lips later that day, it was already immortalized in the annals of social media. I was sure everyone with a Facebook account had seen it. My stomach flip-flopped. Sure, I was massively relieved that there wasn't any trouble. Nothing thrown at them, nothing hateful shouted. But like most big, dramatic moments in her life, she'd felt compelled to do this in front of an audience, and I felt exposed, as though she'd megaphoned our family secret to the whole town.

———

A couple of days before the prom, I hosted a book club night in my home with a few loyal, longtime friends who'd walked with us through more than one family crisis. They knew Abby had come out and let me know they were there for me if I ever wanted to talk.

After a short book discussion, we spent the evening catching up on each other's lives. I was distracted about the upcoming prom and had a hard time joining in the lighthearted banter. When my friend Christy started mildly complaining about how picky her daughter had been while shopping for a prom dress, I interrupted her with a look that made her stop midsentence, waiting for me to explain. I ran to the laundry room and came back with a plastic-wrapped prom dress in each hand—Abby's and her date's—then told them the whole saga of the dramatic song-proposal at school.

"So," I said, "this is *my* current reality. While you're all mildly annoyed with your kids, I'm trying to wrap my head around the fact that my daughter and her date are *both wearing dresses to the prom* and the whole town probably knows about it."

I waited for the outpouring of sympathy, the validation of my resentment, the echoes of my feelings of humiliation.

None came.

Instead, my therapist friend in the book group said, "I want to be like Abby when I grow up."

Everyone laughed. Not at all what I wanted to hear, but in spite of myself, I reluctantly laughed too.

"She's awesome," I admitted, "when she's not airing *your* family business out in public." I felt overly dramatic myself in that moment, determined for them to understand my dilemma. "What if I wasn't ready to talk about this with people? People who don't know us like you all know us. How do I possibly explain all the conflict in my heart about this when I don't even understand it myself?"

Like a good therapist, Jeff answered my question with a question: "Why do you feel like you have to say anything at all?"

I paused. "Well, because people will already know about it from their kids . . . or Facebook."

True to form, he parlayed with another question: "Okay. What makes you think *you* have to tell them anything?"

"Because . . ." I was losing steam. Why *did* I feel like I needed to talk about this?

Jeff said, "The way I see it, this is Abby's story. Let her tell it the way she wants. That's not on you."

Such a simple piece of advice. I felt it go deep and speak to my combination of fear and skewed sense of obligation to "explain" our situation.

Long after my friends left, Jeff's comments stayed with me, bringing to the surface questions I hadn't even considered: Why was I trying to take responsibility for the telling of this entire messy, complicated story? Who gave me that job? Certainly not Abby.

Some part of me believed that if I kept a tight hold on the reins of this narrative, I could control how the public saw our family, me. I could protect the image I wanted people to have of me as a responsible, godly parent. Letting Abby tell it her way felt too risky. My reputation felt at stake—both as a Christian artist with a platform that put me in front of hundreds of churches and as a parent raising my kids according to a standard I claimed to follow. Would other Christian parents think I was a good mom, standing by while Abby fell in love with her friend last year? While she asked a girl to the prom? Technically, she hadn't sought out my permission to do either, but should I have put my foot down and said no to all of it?

In the end, I knew that what made me most uncomfortable with Abby living her new life "loud and proud" was the fear that it would reflect badly on me in some way. As if Abby's story had become all about *me*. I felt ashamed at my small-mindedness, at the value I placed on my own self-protection. Yes, there were aspects to Abby being gay that I needed time to work through—in prayer, in conversations with trusted people in my life, in my study and research of Scripture. But for Abby's sake and mine, I needed to make room for her story to be her own—whatever that looked like. Abby was capable and certainly willing to write her unfolding story, and as Jeff said, it was hers to tell.

My baby was growing up. Abby's senior year was filled with one emotionally wrenching reminder after another that she was becoming her own person and getting ready to fly from the nest. The culminating events came so fast: senior pictures, prom, grad night, finals, last day of school, graduation—there was no time to let it all sink in. Suddenly, her life as a high school student was over.

I shared all of the usual heartbreak with every "senior parent" that year while also trying to readjust my dreams and expectations to fit this new reality that my daughter was gay. It was equal parts terror of the unknown and bittersweet relief that she had been at home with us for at least one last year. We got to do that whole eventful, wild year together. She got to spread her newly outed wings and soar through her senior year without having to hide her true self from us anymore.

When I revisit the pictures I saved from Abby's prom day, it looks different from how I remember it. One of my favorites is a close-up of Abby and her date standing outside in the sunlight, all dressed up, smiling at the camera. Abby is wearing a fire-engine-red gown with her auburn hair swept into a side knot, and they both look so happy and radiant, I wonder how I could have ever thought going to prom wasn't a brilliant idea. Hard to imagine I had been gripped with anxiety leading up to that day, and here she was: smiling, carefree, innocent.

How had I missed that?

The second picture I saved—and framed—from Abby's prom day is of my husband and me, also in the sunlight, also smiling at the camera. We were with the girls and a small group of their friends taking pictures in someone's backyard. What I remember is trying to hold myself together and not weep uncontrollably at the sight of my baby girl all grown up, going to the last dance of her high school years. You'd never know it looking at the photo. My smile is especially big and happy and looks genuinely full of joy. Every time I see it I'm reminded that some moments are bathed in the kind of grace that allows us to rejoice and grieve at the same time.

I wonder if all parents, and especially mamas, see their kids' lives as extensions of their own. When our kids make smart, responsible choices, we feel good about ourselves, not only because it means we did our job right, but because their hearts and brains and DNA reflect so much of *us*. When they take paths we don't understand or agree with, whatever the reasons, we absorb the consequences—perceived or real—along with the shame of feeling like we failed them in some way.

Extricating ourselves from our children's stories as they get older, allowing them to experience the world on their own terms and make their own choices, feels almost unnatural sometimes. But I have to trust that it's the only way they grow into the people they need to become. The paradox of motherhood is that life is constantly forcing us to let go of the very things we want to hold most tightly—our child's well-being, safety, happiness. I've thought a million times that if Abby could just not put herself out there so much, she'd be safe. I keep forgetting that being safe has never been Abby's agenda.

I'm still learning when to lean in and when to step back and watch my daughter's story unfold the way she wants it to. For every time I've wanted to say, "Here's what I think you should do . . . ," she's surprised me with her maturity, her old-soul wisdom, and most of all, her fearlessness. When I'm able to put aside my misgivings and make room for her to grow into the woman God created her to be, I can see that my daughter has been teaching me all her life how to be brave.

6

picturing you

MAKING ROOM FOR REMEMBERING

a mid the flurry of events that marked Abby's final weeks of high school, I wanted to do something special for her that would commemorate this passage from childhood to adulthood. A gift I hoped she'd remember and treasure always. So what started out as a project I thought I could pull off one afternoon, in a classic overachiever move became one that took several days, two boxes of Kleenex, and *nearly* a trip to the therapist to complete. I assumed it would be a gift for Abby, but it was obvious even before I finished it which of us needed it more.

All credit goes to insomnia for the idea I came up with in the middle of the night, which is when I plan all creative endeavors I'm convinced will be the best thing I will ever accomplish with my life. With Abby's graduation just around the corner, I decided to create a slideshow to show our friends and family at her graduation party. I had a smidge of computer savvy, and this didn't seem *too* complicated. Scan some photos into my MacBook, add music, burn it to a disc we could pop it into the DVD player? Easy peasy.

Our family needed this. I needed this, more than I knew. It had been a rough couple of years, filled with enough heavy, major life events to fill an entire season of gripping television drama. Now it was time to celebrate our girl's rite of passage from childhood to adulthood; a party would do us all good. A slideshow shouldn't take more than a couple of hours to put together, I thought, and besides, *it would be fun*.

Someone should have warned me to proceed with caution. My daughter was about to graduate from high school, likely to leave the nest soon, and had recently told me she was gay. To say that my heart was a wee bit *tender* might not be a strong enough word to describe the wrecked condition I was in. I cried about anything remotely related to mothers and daughters: a TV commercial, a song, a sermon illustration in church. Everything felt triggering, and yet here I was about to dive headlong into a deep pool of memories.

I started the project one morning after Abby left for school. I made myself a cup of strong coffee and dug out photo albums I hadn't looked at in years, bracing myself for the tidal wave of emotion. Page after page, I began revisiting photo-worthy moments in my daughter's life.

Blowing out the candle on her first birthday cake. Grinning at the camera in her blue raincoat and matching umbrella, a wide gap replacing one of her front teeth. Every memory in vivid color and gut-wrenching clarity.

Halfway through the first album, the tears started, and I knew this was going to either completely obliterate what was left of my heart or heal what was broken since Abby came out.

Some mothers say there were clues; they had a premonition or a gut feeling about their child being gay before they came out. Not me. I was sure that the teary confession she was about to deliver on that morning drive to school was that she was pregnant. I was blindsided. This inexplicable information about my child, this anomaly in Abby's genetic makeup or whatever it was, didn't fit into any of the memories I had of her past or visions I had of her future.

Sifting through the photos, I withdrew into a cocoon of grief, overcome by an almost suffocating sadness at the loss of the girl I thought was my daughter, the daughter I had believed for seventeen years was *normal* in every way. This "other" new Abby felt like a stranger walking around in skin I knew as intimately as my own but an identity

I no longer recognized or understood as belonging to me.

Eighteen years before, when the ultrasound technician had rubbed a rollerball across my belly and pointed to a monitor confirming that our second baby was a girl, I stared at her fuzzy outline in awe. Like our firstborn, she was a surprise—we didn't exactly excel at family planning—but we were overjoyed nonetheless. Abby waited two weeks after her due date to arrive on her brother's third birthday. We rejoiced in this double-portion blessing: a boy and a girl, born on the same day!

I paused over a photo of eighteen-month-old Abby sitting in a little red wagon in the pediatric surgery unit at Children's Hospital in Oakland. She was smiling and waving goodbye to us just before undergoing corrective surgery for strabismus in her left eye. The doctors had tried having her wear glasses at just five months old, as hysterical as it was heartbreaking, but it didn't correct her condition. Although I hated putting us both through the trauma of surgery, it worked like a charm. I sent up a heartfelt prayer of thanks to God for those two healthy eyes looking back at me in the photos.

I laughed as another rush of memories came with the parade of Abby's yearly Halloween pictures. At four, she was Dorothy from *The Wizard of Oz*, looking like the poster child for DIY costumes, with red glitter shoes her dad had spray-painted and botched-up bangs courtesy of her preschool friend playing hairdresser. She couldn't have been smiling any bigger, completely oblivious to the bad haircut and homemade shoes.

I stopped at one of the multigenerational, overly posed holiday pics we used to take. I had what my sister calls "mall bangs" that screamed early '90s. The photo showed my grandmother holding a teeny, cross-eyed Abby in a pale blue dress; me sitting beside her; and my mom standing behind me. I marveled at all the DNA code that had passed from mothers to daughters in this photo. We were connected by blood, habits, quirks, health risks, and who knows how many other mysterious similarities.

My heart ached at each of these iterations of Abby. The various hair colors and hairdos, the braces and glasses, the clothing styles. No amount of makeup, masks, costumes, or bad haircuts could hide her mischievous eyes and dimpled cheeks. I'd know that face anywhere.

I'm convinced that one of a mother's superpowers is the ability to look at her child at any age and see what never changes: their essence, being, soul that a mother can always see. Revisiting all of those memories, I felt the cold distance I put between Abby and me since she had come out begin to melt away. In every photo, I saw the same girl she'd always been. I remembered holding her in my arms at six months, at seven, now at seventeen—and it was the same heart beating against mine every time. She had my weak left eye, my dimples, my voice.

Nothing essential about Abby changed when she came out to me—it was me who had pulled away from her, me who had alienated her while I grappled with my confused emotions and changing expectations, me who had questioned whether she was still the same beautiful girl who'd stolen my heart the day she was born.

I knew now why I had taken on this project. It didn't matter about the graduation party or even whether Abby loved it—she'd probably be happier with a card and a wad of cash. This whole process of remembering and reliving was for me. I needed reminding of something that in picture after picture I heard in the line of an old Jonatha Brooke song: *you are so much mine.*

———

Forget *a couple of hours*; I spent several days looking through photo albums for quintessential Abby shots before finally finishing the slideshow. It wasn't Oscar worthy, but it would do. I watched it a hundred times while making it and still couldn't get through it without bawling. I hoped Abby would feel my love for her in it, see that I found her beautiful at every age, and know I was proud of her. All the things that, lately, had been stuck somewhere between my heart and my throat, unsaid.

As all big life events go, graduation day passed way too quickly. The ceremony was a blur of marching yellow and blue robes, and before I could catch my breath, loved ones crowded into our home, nibbling on finger foods and cake, congratulating Abby.

When the party started to wind down, my husband got up to say a few words (getting choked up as he always did in these kinds of settings), and I introduced and started the slideshow. Abby sat on the floor with friends while the adults lined the perimeter of the room, balancing their paper plates gingerly and straining to see the TV.

I tried to read Abby's expressions as each new picture flashed on the screen, hoping for a loving look in my direction that said, "Mom, you did this for me? You love me this much?" But when the slideshow ended and everyone dispersed, Abby got caught up in making plans with her friends to leave for another party.

I pulled her aside, curious to know what she thought.

"Well . . . did you like the slideshow?"

"Yeah, it was fun seeing all those old pics," she said, "even if I was kind of mortified at the Tahoe one. I *hated* that stage. I felt like a whale!"

"What? But you looked so cute!"

She laughed, dismissing my comment and ending the conversation with a quick hug, eager to be off with her friends. "It's fine, Mom. Thanks for all the work you did today."

I was hoping for more—some kind of epic, teary, mother-daughter moment in which we hugged and cried and talked everything out—until it occurred to me that maybe Abby wasn't feeling the need for a heart-to-heart like I was. She just wanted to go be a teenager.

Later in bed, exhaustion enveloping me, I sighed at the events of the past week. Looking through those old photo albums, I realized, gave me the precious opportunity to pause and celebrate my daughter. To time travel for a few days, meeting her over and over again at various ages and stages in her life: the happy wonder (and worry) of pregnancy, the anxious waiting for surgery results, the mayhem of back-to-back birthday parties for two kids born on the same day. When I caught glimpses of my husband and me in those photos, I saw two wide-eyed kids, equal parts overwhelmed and overjoyed at being parents.

It occurred to me that most of the things I'd worried, wondered, and stressed about in those pictures eventually worked themselves out. Some not in the way I would have liked, but as far as I could see, my kids survived their childhood fairly unscathed and turned out all right. Shocking, but it probably wasn't my hand-wringing or worst-case-scenario worrying in the middle of the night that got me through those tough seasons. No, it was usually the steady, slow work of time that eventually brought the wisdom and insight I desperately needed as a young mother.

And I wondered, Could I make room for—and trust—the work of time again? With all of the concerns I had about Abby's future, with all of the questions I had for God? Right now, I could only see this one snapshot of a moment, and it was blurry at that. But the pictures I'd saved through the years, Polaroid vignettes along the lines of my memory, told a different story. A story of change, of growth, of a life in motion.

If life was indeed always moving, then surely this too was only a brief stopping point, a place we passed through on the way to somewhere else. What that somewhere else looked like I didn't know yet. But time had already proven to me, over and over, that most of the things we fear never come to pass. We can spend our lives either imagining the worst or hoping for the best.

Either way, I began to believe that the picture of who Abby was becoming, like all the other photos in those old albums, would reveal itself more clearly over time.

7

circle of trust

MAKING ROOM
FOR NEW COMMUNITY

*t*here's something about an unexpected, life-changing event that brings into sharp focus who your "circle of trust" people are, to steal a phrase from *Meet the Parents*. They're the ones you think of after you've passed through the initial stage of shock and realize, *I need to tell someone*. They're the ones who won't ask a lot of questions, who will love you no matter what, and who will remind you of what normal feels like when life feels anything *but*.

When I first learned Abby was gay, I wasn't sure who I could trust enough with this news. Most of the friends I turned to for support and prayer shared a common faith background with me. During our toughest seasons as a family—when my dad died, when our kids were sick, even when we faced our worst financial hardship—our church friends showed up, offering insight and wisdom from their own similar experiences or simply "agreeing in prayer" with us for whatever the crisis called for. It was in those times, especially, that we felt surrounded and buoyed up by a community that shared our values and stood with us.

I longed for that sense of community in those first tender weeks after Abby came out to us. I wanted to pick up the phone and spill everything to someone who understood what I was going through or at least listened with a sympathetic ear and an open heart. I wanted to pray with a fellow believer—though I didn't know what to pray for—just to feel another person of faith sharing the weight of it with me. I needed to lean into my faith community and draw strength and comfort from their collective support.

But this, I knew, was different. Among my Christian friends, there was no common ground here. None of them had walked this path. Most went to conservative churches similar to mine, where homosexuality wasn't talked about other than in terms of "what the Bible says about it." I had no idea how my church friends would react. Would they be compassionate? Understanding? Willing to listen, to ask questions with me, grieve with me? Or would they pull back, uncomfortable with the conflicted position it put them in with their own beliefs?

I rehearsed imaginary conversations in my head, trying to determine which friends would be "safe" to tell. More than anything, I desperately needed to trust whoever I told—beyond a shadow of a doubt—to love Abby without question or judgment and to respect my wishes for privacy.

The truth is I could hardly make sense of my own reaction, let alone guess how my family and friends would react. My emotions often bounced around from fear to anger to confusion in a single minute, a rubber ball in a pinball machine. I needed someone other than just my husband to talk to. It didn't seem fair to unleash the full force of my turmoil on Abe every time he walked through the door—he was fighting his own battles too. But who *could* I bring into such an intensely emotional storm with me? It seemed like a lot to ask, even of my closest friends.

Heart-to-heart talks, open communication, those things were my strong suits. When the people I loved struggled through big life issues, I was good at listening and providing feedback, helping them clarify their messy feelings and irrational emotions. But this situation seemed to suck the words and reason right out of me. The fears I had about Abby were guttural, hard to articulate, and they came out mostly as sobs and sighs. Any words I could find about it sounded a little crazy and extreme even to my own ears, revealing my ignorance, my anger, my despair. Not exactly the stuff of casual conversations over coffee.

Ultimately, the decision to make room for others in that messy, emotional space came down to a simple (but not easy) choice: I could risk being seen and possibly rejected by people I loved, or I could put up walls and isolate myself. My introvert self tried to convince me I didn't need anyone, that I'd be better off dealing with it alone, but experience told me otherwise. I knew those tender, close-to-the-bone, hard-to-talk-about things often lost their shaming power when I was vulnerable enough to share them with someone. It would be scary, but the alternative of walking through it alone was unbearable to me.

I figured I'd start with a very tight circle—my sister and a kindred-soul friend I'd known for several years. Both were sensitive listeners and go-to confidants any time I needed to talk. I called each of them that first week, and as expected, our conversations were epic-length sobfests punctuated by pockets of silence and quiet sighs. I found that after holding in the news so tightly, telling the closest women in my life felt like a huge exhale. The relief was almost physical, leaning into their kindness and empathy. The first small glimmers of hope sparked inside of me, suggesting there might be room for supporting and understanding people in what would otherwise have been a lonely experience.

But to widen the circle of trust was something altogether different.

In small-town communities like mine, where you run into church friends daily, there's an element of shaming that can happen. And a kind of silence encouraged. I hated the thought of being the person with a family problem, the talk of our small town. "Staci *who*? Oh, right, the one with the gay daughter"—as if that had become my identity now. I wanted to be seen as the artsy musician, the talented wife to a funny, loving husband. The hip, smart mom to two great kids. The last thing I wanted was that deadly small-town sympathy rarely verbalized but always lingering in the air, where people at the local coffee shop get awkward around you and the people in your church feel sorry for you as the victim of some awful tragedy—because that's exactly how most Christians I knew viewed my situation.

Early on, I felt like it was a tragedy myself, which is why I was conflicted about people finding out. Most Christians I knew held strong beliefs about the topic but hadn't thought through the implications of how those beliefs affected real people. Understandably, most of them had no idea how to talk about what it was like to have a gay child, and I began to dread having conversations about it with Christians. I saw in their faces a mix of pity and compassion, as though I'd just told them my baby had Down syndrome or my teenager was in drug rehab. It was usually only a matter of seconds before the inevitable look came with the inevitable words, "I'll be praying for her."

It became clear that for most people who offered up those words, that meant praying for Abby to change, to come around to the truth, to make a choice to be straight. Or the biggie: for God to heal her. But that "promised prayer" also covered for other things like judgment, toeing the party line of church teaching, self-righteousness, and even disgust. Most Christian communities I was familiar with didn't make room for deeper conversations about this topic or for an openness to explore the human side I was experiencing. It was simply an *issue* they were unequivocally against.

In the beginning, it was easy to join my brothers and sisters in Christ when they said they were praying for Abby. Wasn't that what I longed for—the solidarity of prayerfully agreeing together in community? But with time and in discerning what people actually meant by those kinds of prayers, I found that I needed to stop saying them. I became aware of the false ground and underlying assumptions those seemingly well-intentioned prayers were based on—that Abby was broken or flawed and needed fixing. No matter how subtle or well hidden that underlying message was, I didn't want it to seep into my conversations about or with my daughter.

I began to realize at a deep-down gut level that loving Abby *unconditionally* meant not seeing her being gay as a mistake on God's part or a willful decision to sin on hers.

Once I made room for that shift in my understanding and acceptance of Abby, conversations with a lot of my Christian friends hit an impasse point. While the message I heard was that the right response to Abby being gay was to *love her no matter what*, for most, that meant convincing her it was wrong. The phrase was often followed by the well-worn phrases "we can't condone sin" or "we have to stand up for truth." Both signaled the inevitable churn in the pit of my stomach at the options in front of me: I could either assert my difference of opinion and turn the conversation into an awkward debate or shut my mouth and pretend to agree.

Soon, I learned to detect all the kind, well-intentioned, subtle ways people said, "Your daughter needs fixing." And while I saw it fit within a framework I was raised with and knew well, it no longer fit the reality I was experiencing.

Throughout that time, I was working through the theology. Though more clarity would come as the months and years unfolded, I was still uncertain about how to understand particular Bible verses and the bigger questions regarding marriage and what it meant to be gay and created in God's image. But one thing I knew for sure, I wasn't going to keep trying to "pray the gay away."

Up until that point, my Christian community had been a place where I felt supported and understood, where I shared the same hopes and prayers for myself and for my children with the people I sat next to in church. We were all there because we recognized we were *sinners saved by grace*, learning to love God and one another. There was room for everyone, I thought.

Now with more clarity, I saw that for most Christians I knew, *everyone* didn't include Abby. In their eyes, she wasn't saved by grace; she was living in sin. Because of that, she wasn't free to serve or lead with her gifts in those places; she didn't have the same right to love and lifelong companionship as their children. The injustice felt suffocating, making it increasingly difficult to stay in places I once felt comfortable.

Looking back now, I understand why I found the company of my nonchurch friends so refreshingly honest and liberating.

Two women, Steph and Christy, were a much-welcomed addition to my expanding little community. Neither of them was connected to my church life. We all had kids in public school together, and as our children became teenagers and we faced some of the same challenges in raising them, we turned to each other for support in the trenches. Along with a casual monthly book club, we started meeting on Saturday mornings at our local Peet's Coffee just to chat, laugh, and generally commiserate about parenting and life. Those coffee dates were a staple on my calendar by the time Abby came out, and they became an unexpected lifeline for me in the months that followed.

When I first told them about Abby coming out—from our tearful conversation in the car to the conflicted emotions I was wrestling with—both listened with nods and tears.

Christy, quick to encourage, squeezed my hand. "I can't imagine what you're going through. But you know how much I love Abby, and as far as I'm concerned, this changes absolutely nothing."

Steph's response was more pragmatic and laced with her typical dry humor: "Whew. At least she isn't pregnant," which somehow got us all howling, laughter lightening the load.

They understood that having a gay daughter was a hard thing to process on more than one level and were sympathetic to my struggle to come to terms with it. But unlike most Christians I knew, they accepted Abby's sexual orientation as something that had nothing to do with right or wrong, moral or immoral. They simply accepted it as part of who she was.

This was a new concept for me, and I found that talking about it without the added "religious weight" was incredibly freeing. Their open-hearted, nonjudgmental acceptance gave me space to open up and be as real and raw as I needed to be about the day-to-day human aspects of parenting a gay teen.

I wondered how something so basic could be missing in a community of faith—an authentic and soul-nourishing friendship. But it was an old pattern I recognized among Christians: rushing past doubt, hurt, grief, to offer advice and prayer and make sense of it all. I knew it was well meant—that instinct to offer comfort to someone in crisis by quoting a Bible verse about how God has things under control. But in the middle of emotional or spiritual turmoil, I realized the need for someone to sit with me in the silence and in the questions, to acknowledge that life can be excruciatingly hard, and to not interject a single piece of advice, however spiritually uplifting they believe it is. And if they couldn't manage that, then they should *just bring food*.

My coffee dates with Steph and Christy involved food and other kinds of soul-nourishing I needed and saved me from an otherwise lonely season.

The truth is, both my husband and I felt isolated from our spiritual tribe. Telling other Christians about this sensitive and challenging part of our story was (and still is in many circles) a risk because people have widely differing beliefs and opinions about this topic, and they often feel compelled to tell us exactly what those are. We knew most of our church friends didn't understand Abby being *openly* out, as she was from the get-go, and I'm sure it was a surprise and a disappointment for them that we accepted this about her.

We understood, to some extent, how that kind of acceptance was uncharted waters for most Christians we knew. They either weren't willing or weren't able, in good conscience, to get into the boat with us. But it was a disappointing, disorienting experience to have people once warm and comfortable around us suddenly get quiet and withdraw when we talked about our daughter. Their silence felt like a door shutting in our faces, making us outsiders in our own community.

At the same time, we witnessed something beautiful happening as we started to open up more about Abby. Some of our Christian friends reached out to tell us that our story had inspired them to do some soul-searching of their own, to examine their beliefs in light of what they were seeing us live out with our daughter. They told us how our acceptance of Abby made them rethink how they'd respond if their child came out.

Whether these friends were motivated by a desire to show solidarity with us (against what felt like an overwhelming majority of Christians who disagreed with our stance) or simply wanted to better understand our hearts and our process, we were beyond grateful for the love we felt from them. To have fellow travelers on this journey was a gift I didn't anticipate.

One such unexpected gift came in the form of a phone call one afternoon. At the end of a long stretch of wondering if anyone understood these unique and sometimes difficult waters we were navigating, my friend Jerran called, simply to say, "We're with you." I made some joke about not having a clue where we were going, but hey, welcome aboard, then asked him to tell me more. That day, especially, I needed to hear the words.

Kindly, he unpacked how he understood this solidarity: "We're watching you do this, and we're grateful to have people in our life showing us what it looks like. I know this is costing you, and not everyone will understand. But any one of us could have a child who comes out, and watching you decide to accept Abby right where she is and not try to change her or shame her or correct her has been eye-opening and inspiring. Thank you for being vulnerable enough to share it with us. I want you to know we're with you."

I choked up. His words felt like a hot compress on my church-wounded heart.

It would have been easier to not talk about this aspect of my life. I could have chosen to live in harmony with the majority of my Christian friends and colleagues by staying quiet about a topic that, after all, didn't impact most people anyway. No one needed to know what my views were about my daughter's sexual orientation, and really, it wasn't their business to begin with. Or that's what I tried to tell myself when I got weary of having hard conversations with Christians. But life kept interrupting, proving to me over and over that this *was* impacting other lives, lots of them.

It was a revelation to me that ours wasn't the only Christian family walking through this, that others were longing to be heard and understood, seen and not rejected by their communities. Friends who needed a safe person to talk to reached out with their stories: "Our son wants to go through transitional surgery . . . ," "Our daughter attempted suicide last night, too scared to tell us she's been seeing a girl . . . ," "My son came out to me, but he's afraid to tell his father . . . ," and on and on and on.

I know what a relief it is in those situations just to hear someone say, "I understand." To know we were fellow members of this unique club and, thank God, we had each other.

Slowly and by turns painfully and miraculously, my little circle of trust expanded to make room for friends inside and outside of the church who stood with me in a space that sometimes felt like spiritual limbo. For every awkward, uncomfortable encounter I've had with Christians who felt compelled to avoid truly listening, to quote the Bible, and to correct my theology, there have been deep, rich, spiritually nourishing conversations with people who wanted to understand and were willing to acknowledge the complexities of our situation. They're the ones who continue to show us over and over again what a loving community looks like.

8

the BLTs

MAKING ROOM FOR LAUGHTER

e very family has a kind of chemistry, a mixture of light and dark, optimism and pessimism, seriousness and levity, that balances out family life when it's all working and feels a little off-kilter when it's not. In our case, having *really* different personality styles under one roof has always kept things interesting, and I became aware of how fragile that balance was and how easy it was to upset in the months after Abby came out to us.

My family loves humor, and at the risk of being judged, I'm going to be honest and admit we like it a little off color. We like jokes about slightly inappropriate things you're not supposed to laugh at, which usually triggers some riffing and spinoff jokes that result in yet more laughter over the plain wrongness of laughing about something you're not supposed to joke about. The whole thing goes downhill so fast you don't have time to stop it.

Dutifully, I've tried, I really have, to refine my family's taste in humor over the years, but my kids come by it honestly. My husband's humor defies taming and defining. It's sideways, lowball, out of left field, sarcastic, and sometimes so obscure that literally no one gets it but him. He's fine with that. He thinks it's proof that he's so funny his jokes can't be decoded or explained. Sometimes all we can do is laugh *at* him, and he's okay with that, too, because if there's one thing Abe lives and breathes for, it's to make us laugh.

In the rough patches we've gone through as a family, laughter has been our escape hatch, our release valve, a way to let out pent-up pressure and clear the air. A good laugh somehow opens up the space between us and allows us to get a little more honest, be a little more vulnerable and tender with each other. Some families experience this when they watch sports together or do something outdoors—it's a collective sigh, a stress reliever.

Being married to someone who makes me laugh daily has its perks. Abe surprises me with his observations, his take on things, and especially his out-of-the-box, irreverent humor. I still, after all these years, don't see it coming most of the time. He looks at the world, communicates, and thinks so differently than me it's a wonder we ended up together and lasted this long. Or maybe it's exactly why.

I knew this when I married him. Even when we were teenagers, I was the straight man in his comedy act. I was earnest; he was sarcastic. I was the good girl; he was the bad boy. I was the wall-flower; he was the life of the party. When we were dating, our phone calls consisted of 80 percent gig-gling (mine) and 20 percent actual conversation.

It worked, I'm convinced, partly because even though I was a serious person, part of me secretly wished I could get away with the outrageous things he said and did. When we were dating, it was always a little thrilling to be around Abe; he didn't act like anyone in my family, or anyone I knew, for that matter. He was full of surprises. And I think a small part of *him* secretly wanted to be reined in by my serious nature—at least that's what I've been telling myself for the past thirty years.

We used to play up our differences onstage when we started playing music together in our twenties and discovered that it worked great with audiences. I was the deep artist who pondered the meaning of life with poetic lyrics; he was the down-to-earth guy next door who served up frank humor in plain English. He loved to interrupt my heartfelt song introductions with completely ran-dom comments, like, "Hey, lighting guy, can you turn down these spots a little? I feel like a rotis-serie chicken up here." Or one of his regular go-tos,

"People, when we're done here, will you please go buy my wife's CDs? My kids need to go to college." Maybe you had to be there, but it worked. I'd feign horror and embarrassment; the audience loved it.

When our kids got old enough to understand his humor (to the extent that anyone *could*), I was relieved to finally have a couple of inside witnesses to his brand of crazy. Over the years, the kids and I have collected a huge catalog of material on Abe that has us finishing each other's sentences, roaring in laughter, or rolling our eyes in mock disgust. Usually, the funniest stories involve Abe not trying to be funny at all. He sometimes has this blustery, cocky, father-knows-all bravado about him, when he's joking and when he's not, so you're never quite sure where he's coming from.

One time we drove seven hours to Los Angeles to take the kids to Disneyland and ended up circling a several-block loop in the dark for over an hour looking for our hotel. We had the street address, 601, but the hotel was set so far back from the road we kept missing it every time we drove past it. We'd been in the car all day, and everyone's fuse was short. When it was my turn to drive, I slowed down to a crawl to take another pass around the route we'd been driving for what felt like days. At that slow pace—lo and behold—we spotted a tiny sign at the entrance of a driveway lit with the numbers 601. Before anyone could even breathe a sigh of relief, Abe declared in his confident-bordering-on-I-told-you-so voice, "Yep. Six-oh-one," like he'd known it was there all along. It was so preposterously, ridiculously *him* we all roared with laughter. To this day, when he thinks he knows something and doesn't, one of us will imitate his cocky "Six-oh-one," and we'll all lose it.

The only time there's been a pause on the humor button in our house was after Abby came out. It was hard on everyone, but a particularly painful silence fell between Abe and Abby, who'd been communicating through humor since she was a little girl. The two shared a love of specific kinds of humor: goofy, nonsense songs made up on the spot (extra points if they rhymed), lines from comedies (extra points if it was a Jack Black or Will Ferrell movie), and the mother of all humor, sarcasm. They also shared a special gift for stretching out a joke long past the point that anyone else found it funny.

If Abby fell into a bad mood, depressed or angry over something, it was her dad's lighthearted, silly banter more than my sympathetic talks that pulled her out. I was grateful for the upbeat energy he brought to heavy conversations. He had a way of finding something funny even in the gloomiest situations and making mundane, drudgery tasks fun. Abby adored that about her dad. Laughter was their love language, and without it, their conversations felt uncharacteristically strained and polite—like two actors following a script.

For Abe, whose whole personhood was wired to speak his mind unfiltered and whose primary method of communicating was humor, having a gay daughter presented unique challenges. He had questions. He had concerns. He had opinions. How much could he say and not be offensive? How far was too far? Not a person normally given to long bouts of self-reflection, these were questions he was not used to asking himself—especially not regarding Abby, his partner in joking crime.

He and I talked about this but only when Abby wasn't around. With me, he could blow off steam and even joke about the things he was curious about or that weighed heavily on his mind. With Abby, though, his jokes could sometimes have a dark side, revealing the resentment or disappointment behind them. Until he could address the root fears and attitudes where that dark humor was coming from, he stayed quiet, not wanting to risk hurting Abby.

But as the tension between them became too much to bear, he decided the only way he could know how far was too far was to start testing the waters, one joke at a time. So when the humor did finally come back, like anything new, it began with baby steps.

Heading into the Christmas season, several months after Abby had come out to us, I repeated my time-honored tradition of asking our kids to make out a Christmas wish list. When they were little, I would sit them at the kitchen table with the latest Target or Toys"R"Us ad and a Sharpie, telling them to circle which toys they wanted. I'm not proud of this parenting technique. I'm sure it fostered an unhealthy level of holiday consumerism, but it got the job done.

Now that they were older, we didn't do that much, but old habits die hard. One Sunday morning we were visiting my parents, and Abby sat on the couch next to her dad flipping through a Target Christmas catalog. Maybe it was the shared memory that made him bold, maybe it was the casual closeness of their shoulders touching, but when she turned to a page showing a pair of preteen girls' underpants that read "I Heart Boys" on the bottom, Abe pointed to them and said casually, "Why don't you add those to your list, Abby?"

Like a slow-motion movie scene, we all stopped talking and turned to look at him for half a second to make sure he was going for a laugh: after all, this would be the first time he'd made an outright joke in front of Abby about her being gay. *Could* he? And in front of my conservative Christian parents, no less? I'd be surprised if he chose *this* moment to break the ice.

Sure enough, we saw the familiar mischievous glint in his eye, and all of us, my parents included, howled. It was one of those belly laughs that hit us on so many levels we didn't know what we were laughing at—the joke itself or the sheer relief of finally being able to laugh about something that had been off-limits and heavy for so long. That split second of comic relief eased away months of tension. Suddenly, I felt hopeful their relationship could be restored to its old self again.

I had almost gotten used to the heaviness around the house; it felt like forever since we all laughed like we used to. Not only had Abe been unusually quiet, but with Zach out on his own now, I missed the silly sibling banter between him and

Abby—arguing over pop song lyrics or pointing out cowlicks in their morning bed hair. I counted on it for a good chuckle at least once a day. The four of us had always kept a steady flow of inside family jokes going; it was our unique bloodline, a shared language, and how we connected our past to the present. I didn't realize how much we needed that collective laughter until it went away for a while. I was more than ready for it to make a comeback.

In fact, I knew Abe was getting his comic groove back when he came home from work not long after the underwear comment and told me he'd heard a good lesbian joke that day. I thought I had heard him wrong. I don't remember him using the word *lesbian* before. We seemed to stick with the more generic *gay*.

"A good *what*?"

"Lesbian joke. Remember my clients Ann and Jamie? The gay couple who bought a house from me a couple of years ago?"

"Vaguely."

"They came to see me today about refinancing, and we got to talking—you know, just catching up. I told them about Abby coming out, and the conversation went from a client meeting to a counseling session." My eyes got big, and he laughed.

"It was actually pretty cool. I asked questions, and they helped me understand some things about Abby."

"Really." I was intrigued that he'd opened up about our daughter being gay—to former clients, no less. "Like what?"

"Like, you know how Abby falls head over heels every time she has a crush on someone new? Like she's found The One every time?"

"Yesssssss," I groaned. It was true. Abby was crazy about someone at the moment, and it hadn't been that long since the *last* girl she'd been crushing on. If I heard "But Mom, this one's different . . ." one more time, I was going to scream. Abe and I would raise eyebrows at each other when she said it, but she had always been the all-or-nothing kind.

"Well, apparently that's a lesbian thing," Abe said matter-of-factly.

I stifled a giggle just hearing those words come out of his mouth.

"Really?"

"Yep."

"Wow."

"They told me this joke: What does a lesbian bring on a second date?"

"Um . . . I don't know."

"A U-Haul."

We laughed hard—the laugh of recognition—and it felt good.

He told it to Abby the next time he saw her and was rewarded with a genuine gut laugh, the kind he lived for.

"Oh my gosh, Dad, that's hi*lar*ious. It's so true!"

They both chuckled a bit more. Then he said, "Is that really a thing with girls? It's not just you?"

"Let's just say I know people who literally embody the punch line of that joke. It happens a lot, Dad."

"Dang! Why?"

"I guess because women are intense and emotional, and a lot of them feel ready to commit sooner than guys would in the same situation."

"Hmm. Well, good to know."

And just like that, a conversation opened up that might have been awkward and even offensive if not for a dumb joke, a joke that gave Abe a humorous—if slightly skewed—glimpse into a world he knew almost nothing about. Abby and I could have heart-to-hearts about most of this stuff; we were starting to already, but she and her dad needed humor. It was the key that helped them slip into tight, hard-to-talk-about places. Abe's lightheartedness gave their relationship room to breathe again, to talk through sensitive, touchy subjects without the heaviness of taking everything so seriously.

What was once taboo to joke about became open season. He asked Abby about things I thought were so personal she'd surely get irritated and shut him down. But to her credit, she was always forthright and honest and just as frank in her responses as he was in the questions. And I learned a lot from their exchanges (as I said, I live vicariously through Abe's boldness). Both of them bravely used their humor to laugh about things otherwise unbearably awkward in family discussions.

Recently, my husband and Abby got into a conversation that led to a bizarre discovery that we have since filed under "You Can't Make This Stuff Up."

It started with Abe and Abby realizing that all of her past and present girlfriends were blonde. (I'm sorry. I don't have a better lead-in; that's just how some conversations in my house start.)

"Except for one or two, they've all been blondes," Abby noted.

"I always had a weakness for blondes too," her dad confessed.

"Come to think of it," Abby said, "they've all had a similar build too. Tall and slender, kind of athletic."

"True," Abe chimed in.

Abby started making other connections among the list of girls she'd dated over the years. "They've all been smart. Great writers. Avid readers. More than one was an English teacher."

"Wow. Sounds like Mom!" Abe said.

They both looked at me as though inspecting a specimen. What they saw was a five-foot-six, blonde former English teacher who read a lot and was writing her second book. I added my two cents: "*And* your current girlfriend drives a red VW Jetta, the same car I drove for years . . ."

Abby turned her head slowly back toward Abe, the strange revelation dawning on her. "Wait, Dad, are we saying that you and I like the same . . . *type*?" She could hardly finish her question; it was too weird to say out loud. She covered her mouth in horror.

There was a moment of silence while we processed this odd information that didn't fit into our familiar family landscape. I wasn't sure *how* I felt about this or what to do with it. Apparently, my husband did because he threw his head back and laughed that big, booming laugh of his, clearing away the awkwardness and once again lightening the mood.

In this ongoing adventure of learning how to do life with our gay daughter, humor has been one of the best reminders for me that we're all human. For someone who overanalyzes and overthinks my way through situations I don't understand, laughter gives me permission to let go of the reins for a minute and freely admit I don't have it all figured out. To surrender to the absurd, to the mysteries of life, when logic and reason don't offer any answers.

More times than I can count humor has broken the silence that settles in where fear and misunderstanding threaten to take over. It melts the walls we put up and reveals our soft spots, the vulnerabilities and fears we all share. If one of us is willing to ask a silly question, to fumble around in the dark or get it wrong—even if it's just for a laugh—it makes room for all of us to do the same. And isn't family, ultimately, the place we most want to feel safe, take risks, make mistakes, or just wave our own brand of crazy flag?

True to our odd taste in humor, my family has acquired a few not-for-public jokes on the gay theme. We don't pull them out too often, but there's one especially that has endured over time and still gets a chuckle. While earnestly trying to learn the culturally relevant term for the gay community, Abe kept confusing the order of the letters in *LGBTQ*. Finally, he gave up and settled on the BLTs. I'm sorry to say, the name stuck.

Don't judge us.

And don't say I didn't warn you.

9

just folks

MAKING ROOM FOR PEOPLE
BEYOND THE LABELS

*N*ever underestimate the power of a dumb question. That's the lesson I kept learning from the many awkward conversations I had with Abby in an effort to better understand this new territory of being the parent of a gay teenager. While humor helped open doors to some of the things I wondered and worried about, it was also true that every new insight came with a new set of uncertainties. More questions that required stretching and expanding my old ways of thinking.

Most pressing on my heart was the dilemma of how to fit Abby's sexual orientation within the context of my faith. Some things had become clear—that Abby being gay wasn't simply a phase or a choice and my unwavering belief that God didn't love her any less because she was gay. But I continued to wrestle with the Bible verses that referenced homosexuality and seek out resources that would help me understand those in light of Abby's relationships or the possibility of her getting married one day. The concerns I had about her future were especially troublesome and unsettling to me. I wanted her to be happy and healthy, as any mother would, and also to flourish spiritually and emotionally, in alignment with what God wanted for her life.

Which is why I was saddened but not surprised when after Abby graduated from high school and started becoming more independent, she stopped coming to church with us. My first instinct was to do everything in my power to drag her with us on Sundays—whether she liked it or not. She genuinely enjoyed the sermons and had a few friends at church since junior high, but I could see that after coming out, she felt less at home there. Not so much because she felt judged outright by people, but she was definitely uncomfortable knowing that most of them believed being gay and out was a sinful lifestyle choice on her part. She didn't want to keep being part of a community where she wasn't accepted for who she was and as a result began seeking out a new group of friends, many of whom were also gay.

I understood her reasons, but I was in no way comfortable with the thought of Abby hanging out with mostly gay friends. In fact, it made me a little panicky. The idea of a "gay community" was so far outside my realm of experience or knowledge, I had no clue what to even call this, this group—was it a subculture?—my daughter was suddenly a part of, with its insider language and confusing protocols. I wanted to know everything I could about the people she spent time with, even the things that seemed silly or random on the surface.

For one thing, I was curious about why some of Abby's friends dressed—for lack of a better word—manly and others more feminine. Some wore their hair short with men's style button-up shirts and dark jeans. A couple of them even added a leather jacket to the outfit, completing the look that matched a certain stereotype I had in my mind of the "butch" lesbian. And for reasons I couldn't quite articulate, had always made me feel uncomfortable.

When I asked Abby about it, she seemed a little annoyed at the word *manly* used to describe how some of her friends dressed.

"It's more of an androgynous look, Mom," she corrected me. "Men don't own that look."

"Okay, but I'd still say it's not very feminine. Why do some, um, lesbians (I was still getting used to saying that word out loud) play down their femininity?"

"They wear what they're comfortable in, just like you."

"But why do you think some of your friends are more comfortable in clothes that *look like* men's? I feel like they're making a statement. Am I wrong?"

"Mom, the statement they're making is 'this is what I'm comfortable in.' Don't try to read more into it."

She wasn't budging, but I kept nudging anyway. I was getting closer to my point. A theory I had and wanted to test out.

"So if a gay woman dresses androgynously, does that mean she wants to be the man in the relationship?"

Abby laughed and shook her head at me, the way a grown-up does when a child says something naive.

"It's not really like that, Mom. At least with most of the people I know, there aren't really firmly drawn traditional male and female roles in a lesbian relationship. Just because a gay woman has short hair and wears preppy clothes doesn't mean she's automatically good at math or fixing cars."

When she said it like that, I had to laugh too. I thought about how many times Abby's style had changed throughout the years. For a while, she'd gone through a skater phase: rock band T-shirts, skinny jeans, and Chuck Taylor sneakers—all black, of course. From the back, she looked like a million other teenage girls, or boys.

Still, there was something more, something hard to put into words that I wanted to understand. "Okay, that's fair. But do you think some lesbians feel *safer* dressed in clothes that don't draw attention to their bodies? Almost like they're wanting to avoid male attention altogether?"

She paused for a minute. "Maybe. But sometimes in social situations, it's just a way of identifying themselves, to avoid getting hit on by guys or to signal to other gay women that they're out."

It made a certain kind of sense. And though this was just one conversation, just Abby's perspective on a topic I'm sure had lots of interpretations and opinions, I was glad I kept asking questions. Without consciously realizing it, I was harboring some negative opinions about "certain kinds" of lesbians: they were aggressive, tough, militant. Maybe there was a butch stereotype that continued to persist in lesbian subculture, but obviously, the reality was much more nuanced than I had made room for in my thinking.

Underlying that conversation and others like it was my fear that Abby would be pulled into relationships and experiences she wasn't emotionally prepared to navigate. She was young in ways that seemed tender and impressionable. Sure, she had a driver's license and a part-time job, but she was still balancing on that precarious edge between young woman and older girl—a ripe catch for someone who might influence her negatively. The notion of a gay community, lifestyle, or culture had always seemed a little dangerous and seedy in my imagination, and I feared it would suck her into its clutches.

Mind you, I had almost zero personal experience with actual gay people. I was a product of my times and culture, coming of age in the '80s in conservative Christian circles. Knowing someone who was gay and out was about as common as knowing someone who had time traveled. Even as a teenager living in the San Francisco Bay Area, my understanding of gay culture was formed mostly from what I saw on TV of the annual Pride parade. And like any news story, the louder and more outlandish the characters, the more screen time they got.

It's no wonder those images had absolutely no connection to my reality. No one in my church or friend circles talked openly about gay people. It was all taboo and hush-hush. You heard whispers about people who had left the church to go live "the lifestyle," but I don't remember anyone explaining what that was, exactly. It made for a lot of speculation, jokes, and titillating gossip among us teenagers.

If I had any doubts about whether the rumors I heard about the gay lifestyle were true—that it consisted mostly of rampant promiscuity—the AIDS crisis sealed the deal. When the death toll among gay men was rising and you couldn't turn on the news without hearing about it, an accompanying growing notion among Christian evangelicals was that AIDS was God's punishment on gay people. Especially in the "modern-day Sodom and Gomorrah" of San Francisco. If there were compassionate, protesting voices raised against this belief, they weren't reaching my circles with much force or regularity. Between the messages and the silence, what came through was clear: *those people* deserved whatever punishment they got.

When I was a teenager, my church youth group went "street witnessing" in some of San Francisco's sketchiest neighborhoods. Although I willingly participated in handing out tracts—miniature comic books containing Bible verses and instructions for how to become a Christian—I was just as terrified by the occasional gay couples we'd encounter as I was the homeless people lying on door stoops. With a mixture of fascination and disgust, I'd wave a tract in their direction, trying not to make eye contact. I can't imagine anyone on those streets witnessing Christ's love through my thinly veiled horror.

In my twenties, I could count on one hand the number of gay people I knew personally. It wasn't until I was in my thirties and early forties that I began having friends who I knew to be gay and out. They came into my life a few years before Abby came out to us, in the usual way friends do—through mutual friends, interests. A couple of them were from church backgrounds similar to my own, and I knew they still had deeply held convictions regarding their faith. Before meeting and getting to know them, I never considered the idea that a gay person could be a Christian.

But old stereotypes from my past persisted, and when my newly out daughter started spending more time with her gay friends and less time at church, my instinct was to circle the wagons in order to protect her from the dangers I feared would be awaiting her. I just wasn't sure what those dangers were, exactly.

The "gay agenda" was a buzz phrase circulating in Christian culture starting around the '90s—and I wondered now, twenty years later, if it was still a thing. If so, did it involve trying to recruit innocents like Abby for their cause? And what was their cause, exactly? Were they out to destroy the moral values our family stood for, like some of the articles I remember reading suggested? More to my own personal fears, I wondered if some of the older girls Abby hung out with might prey on her, sexually or otherwise. Would she become brainwashed and eventually be persuaded to leave her home, her faith, her family?

My paranoia is almost laughable to me now, and even at the time, some of these questions sounded ridiculous in my own head, but I felt like an outsider in her world. I didn't know what was true and what was my own imagination. Fear of the unknown fueled my worry. I hated thinking about the chasm that could grow between my daughter and me if those irrational fears took over. If I allowed myself to believe that in coming out, my daughter had become something other than the Abby I'd always known and loved, that she had become one of *them*, I knew I'd lose her. I couldn't bear the thought of it.

Someone wise once said if you want to build a bridge, you have to spend time on both sides you're trying to connect. Obviously, separating myself from Abby's growing new community of friends wasn't going to help me cross my gulf of fear, so I decided to take baby steps toward it instead. As usual, those steps were at first awkward and uncomfortable.

While my former conservative-Christian self couldn't have imagined darkening the door of a gay bar, that's exactly what I did one evening when Abby invited me to come and hear her sing at a club. Though not yet twenty-one, she had been performing for a while at a few local open mic nights. The customers at this particular club happened to be mostly lesbians—I said yes before I could chicken out. Granted, I was nervous and about as far out of my element as I could get. I'm sure everything about my sensible outfit and self-conscious demeanor screamed, *Heterosexual Christian mom!*—but despite my discomfort, I actually managed to enjoy myself.

Sitting at a table with a few of Abby's friends, I mostly listened as they laughed and talked about school, work, relationships—the usual stuff. They were sensitive to my newbie status in their world and graciously invited me into the conversation at various points. Gradually, I felt the tension in my body relax as an unexpected realization sunk in: I was among friends. I didn't see any weirdos or freaks, no one acting inappropriately or out of control: just a handful of young women listening to music and having a few drinks with friends.

That evening proved to be a small but profound revelation that opened up my thinking about what a "gay community" looked like. As far as I could tell, there was no sinister or hidden agenda underlying the conversations, just the same desire for belonging and companionship you'd expect to see in any community. Yes, it would take me a while to get used to seeing women being affectionate with one another the way men and women were, but the more time I spent in those casual settings with Abby and her friends, the more I learned to see them as people beyond just a label or category.

———

Around that time, I reached out to a friend, seeking insight about some of my questions and concerns. Laura, a lawyer living in Boston with her partner of over ten years, was one of the two friends I had at the time whom I knew to be Christian and also gay. We shared mutual friends and, a couple of years before, had done an Annie Dillard book study together online, giving me a glimpse into her wisdom, kindness, and spiritual maturity.

Not only did she have something in common with Abby; like me, Laura was in a committed, monogamous relationship, which spoke volumes to me of shared values and stability. Because she was a Christian, I knew Laura and I shared a language with which I could express my honest opinions and concerns. When I nervously hit "send" on my first email, Abby was spending more time with her new gay friends, and I wondered if this was normal and what Laura's take was on "gay culture."

Her reply was reassuring: "I would expect Abby to have a significant number of gay friends. . . . I found a bonding in being with people who understood and accepted that part of me, who had also experienced some of the same difficulties that I had. There is a feeling that you can be who you are without judgment, and it's freeing to begin to sort through thoughts and emotions."

It made sense. And I hadn't even thought about the shared difficulty part. I knew some of Abby's friends had come out to their own families and hadn't experienced the kind of acceptance Abby had. Even without the added weight of a conservative faith background, it was a heavy undertaking for a young person to tell their parents and friends they were gay. I could see how the shared experience of going through that would create a bond among Abby's friends.

Laura went on to write, "The gay culture you see on TV and that's generally depicted in society truly is stereotypical and doesn't represent most gay/lesbian people I know. I would expect that the girls Abby is hanging around are just girls trying to figure themselves out too, and I would not expect them to be (as a group) predatory."

Her phrase "just girls trying to figure themselves out" struck a chord and made me choke up unexpectedly. I hadn't thought of that either. In my late teens, I remember facing big, grown-up decisions about college and what to do with my life, feeling overwhelmed and unsure of where I fit into the world. Some of Abby's new friends were around that age and probably going through similar transitions into adulthood, trying to find their own path. Why had I feared that just because they were gay they would be a negative influence?

At the core of my questioning was a nagging, constant worry that the rift between Abby's new community of gay friends and her faith upbringing would split her in two and that she would be lost to us. It was one of my biggest torments since day one of her coming out. Laura replied with honesty and hard-earned insight from her own experience: "There will inevitably be some ambiguities for you and her if she does interact more with gay people or has a gay relationship or interacts with what's represented as gay 'culture.' Are there unsavory parts to it? Yes. But there's also a lot of realness and hurt and freedom of expression and beauty there too . . . you have to pick and choose, and in doing so, find out who you are."

Her response made me think more deeply about my own biases. Of *course* my daughter's new life would be filled with all kinds of people, and she would have to use good judgment about which ones were safe or potentially toxic and harmful. That would be true if she weren't gay too. Every mother is anxious about her child's emotional and physical safety as they become more independent and spend less time at home and more time with friends. I'd always known Abby to be a good judge of character in her friendship choices. Making sinister assumptions about her gay friends that I didn't about her "straight" ones was unfair.

Those conversations with Laura and the time I spent with Abby's new friends helped make room for the real people behind the "LGBTQ" label that now applied to my own daughter. At first, I had an almost physical reaction to that label and didn't feel at all comfortable using it. "LGBTQ" sounded more like a political agenda to me than a group of people. Most evangelical Christians I heard use it made "those people" out to be a threat to my morals, my family, my way of life. The truth is, I didn't see anything dangerous or subversive about Abby's new friend community, regardless of what label someone attached to them.

As I continued to ask questions, have conversations, and think through some of my wrong assumptions about the LGBTQ community, a puzzling story from the Bible came to my attention. One I'd grown up hearing in church but never given much thought to. Revisiting it now, I was struck by how profoundly it spoke to my heart in this situation.

The story describes a follower of Jesus, the apostle Peter, having a strange vision three times in a row of a white sheet descending from the sky filled with all sorts of birds and animals considered "unclean" by Jewish dietary laws. He hears a voice from heaven telling him to kill and eat the animals, but he protests, saying he's never eaten anything unclean. The voice replies, "Do not call anything impure that God has made clean." Immediately after having these three identical visions, Peter is summoned to the house of a Roman guard, a Gentile (i.e., someone considered an "unclean" outsider), forbidden by Old Testament law for Jews to associate with. With the understanding from his visions, Peter agrees to go into the man's house and baptize him. What he explains to his Jewish community on his return is that no one is considered unclean according to God. "They have received the Holy Spirit just as we have," the book of Acts records Peter explaining to those shocked by his actions (10:47).

I thought about the ways my upbringing, religious culture, and the media had shaped my views about gay people, and I imagined what I felt was similar to what the Jews felt about the Gentiles. Distrustful of them, morally superior to them, threatened or disgusted by their "otherness." Entering the home of a Gentile couldn't have been easy for Peter, just as walking into a gay bar wasn't for me. I had to look past the stereotypes that had been filtering my perspective for decades and see real faces. People with names, personalities, families. The message in the story and that night to me in the bar was clear: *all* were loved and considered clean by God.

It's difficult to admit that until Abby came out, I didn't think about biases I'd harbored about gay people since as far back as childhood. I never imagined the "LGBTQ community" could include kids like mine, from families like ours. Kids who were just trying to figure out their lives, find their path, make their parents proud. I watched Abby's gay and nongay friends alike go through similar life experiences: auditioning for their dream gigs, scraping to make ends meet in college, struggling through breakups, moving away from home, getting their first full-time jobs. The details varied, but all of them were just young people trying to make the awkward leap into adulthood the best way they knew how.

The distinctions between "us" and "them" I once thought to be clearly defined became blurry. I saw

that people are far more alike than we are different. One of my favorite lines from Harper Lee's
To Kill a Mockingbird is when Scout says, "I think
there's just one kind of folks. Folks." I've tried to
keep these words close to my heart as Abby has
moved in and out of friendships and relationships
with people I've grown to love. It's hard to imagine I was once worried about her spending time
with these LGBTQ "folks." I've sat across tables from
them, laughed with them, cried with them, and
made room for their stories in my heart. My life is
bigger and more beautiful because they are in it.

10

uninvited

MAKING ROOM FOR DIFFERENCES

*e*ven as my heart was opening up to new ways of understanding my daughter and her friends, the churches I was attending and working in still held traditional views about homosexuality. To be "out" and gay, they said, was to live in opposition to what the Bible taught. But I was starting to see cracks where I once saw rock-solid truth behind that teaching. In my research and in my day-to-day life with Abby, something about this wasn't making sense anymore. In my private life, I was working through the questions in prayer, conversations with friends, and an intentional, thorough study of Scripture and other helpful resources.

In my public life, I was doing what I'd been doing for over twenty years: recording albums and traveling, leading worship, doing concerts, and speaking at various churches and Christian events. At times, it felt like I was living a double life—working and serving in places that held to a belief I wasn't sure I agreed with anymore. I felt conflicted on those rare occasions when I shared publicly about having a gay daughter, but I wasn't hiding it either. In general, my introvert MO was to avoid conflict and confrontational conversations whenever possible.

Still, I knew the topic was bound to come up sooner or later.

It happened in a phone call that took an unexpected turn. The director of a women's group—Emma, I'll call her—contacted me from a large church where I had sung multiple times over a period of several years. I had a long-standing professional relationship with this church, one I valued greatly, as those kinds of repeat bookings were how I made my living. I was scheduled to sing at one of their events later that month, and I assumed she was calling to firm up the details. It didn't take long to realize something was off.

"Do you have a moment?" she said. "I'm calling about the event here next month. I understand you were invited to be our special musical guest."

"Yes! I'm looking forward to it."

"Right . . . Well, um . . ." She paused and let her voice trail off, like she wasn't sure how to proceed. A beat of awkward silence filled the line between us. "I'm afraid I'm calling to . . ." Another pause.

This was uncharacteristic of Emma. In our past interactions, she'd always been cheery and articulate and especially good at keeping a conversation rolling.

She got to her point: "I'm afraid I have to uninvite you as our musical guest."

My mind tried to make sense of her words. Her tone was polite, but *uninvite* stung, like a slap. I was momentarily silenced, racking my brain for all the possible reasons I could be *uninvited* to an event less than a month away by a church I had a strong relationship with. Had they overspent their budget? I could see how that *would* be awkward to explain. Had the event been unexpectedly canceled?

"Okay . . ." I paused, leaving her an opening to explain.

"It's, um, come to our attention . . . We received an email . . . someone . . . er—"

She was struggling, and my radar was picking up a bad signal. I just couldn't put my finger on the source of it yet. She continued, hesitantly: "Apparently, there was . . . a certain blog post you wrote . . . about your daughter?"

And there it was. A punch in the gut even before I knew where this was going.

I'd written a blog post: "What I Learned about Love When My Daughter Came Out." In the post, I wrote about the journey my heart made in coming to terms with Abby being gay. The conclusion I came to in the piece—that it was not fundamentally wrong or sinful to be gay—made me a minority among conservative evangelicals. I knew there were a lot of Christians who wouldn't share my decision to accept Abby's sexual identity without qualifying it as something that needed changing or overcoming. Posting it on my website was the first step I'd taken toward publicly supporting my daughter.

"Did you read it?" I asked Emma.

"I did. I thought it was well-written and clearly from the perspective of a mother who loves her daughter very much."

"Thank you," I answered cautiously. "I'm glad you got that impression. It was my attempt to explain what the experience has taught me about love."

"Yes, yes, of course . . ."

"I guess I'm not understanding what the problem is."

"It's just that . . . Some of the things you wrote . . . Um, revealed . . . your views on homosexuality . . . that don't . . . align with our church." Then she added, inexplicably, "We want this to be a unifying event . . ."

Blood rushed to my face, and my heart pounded hard against my chest. Now I understood. Shame started to rise up inside of me like bile. *But you've done nothing wrong*, I told myself.

"I'm sorry, but what does this have to do with me singing at your event?" I spoke slowly and carefully, trying to keep the rising emotion out of my voice. "Are you saying that because of an email from one person I'm no longer welcome to sing at your church?"

Silence for a beat. Then quietly she said, "It's just that . . . it wouldn't have been the *only* email."

So. She had made up her mind.

I took a breath. Trying again to keep my voice from shaking, I moved forward. "For over ten years, I've shared my heart and my music with your women, and I've never once heard any negative feedback. Is *this* how you're choosing to end that relationship?"

I hardly ever say dramatic things like that. I loathe confrontation, and this whole conversation felt like a ten on my anxiety scale. But here I was, laying my heart and professional reputation on the table.

"I'm sorry . . . It's just . . . We can't support . . . We really want this to be a unifying event."

I still had no idea why she kept using *unifying event* in her reasoning. Was she afraid that me singing a few songs with my guitar was going to cause such an uproar of division they had to ban me from their stage? The thought was almost comical, me with my folky-pop songs about how God was working in my life. I wanted to press her on it, ask her what she meant, but I was already teetering between outrage and humiliation. I didn't want to completely lose it on the phone. Better to end the conversation.

"That's disappointing. I don't think there's anything left for me to say."

"Again, I'm so sorry."

I hung up, staring out the window, too stunned to even blink for a few moments. Slowly, I felt my shock begin to morph into indignation and gradually, flat-out anger. The injustice of it. The ridiculous hypocrisy of it. The short-sightedness. The insensitivity. And just the illogical thinking behind the decision to "uninvite" me. After all, I'd been booked to *sing*, not give a lecture on homosexuality! What could possibly be the danger in that?

I had fostered a solid reputation with hundreds of churches over several years of experience as a musician, speaker, and worship leader. I believed I belonged in these particular arenas; I had the credentials and the expertise. A core message I often spoke about and tried to live out in my life was the belief that all of us should nurture, develop, and invest our gifts and talents, and I had even spoken on that topic at Emma's church. To be uninvited from this event, not because I lacked ability or professionalism or had a lapse in moral character, but because I believed that my daughter was loved and accepted by God just as she was felt like the worst kind of betrayal.

Underneath the anger, threatening to rise to the surface again, was shame. And though I continued to remind myself I'd done nothing wrong, shame whispered that I was no longer worthy of standing on this church's stage. No longer respected for the gifts and talents I had to offer. No longer fit to serve alongside their ministry leaders. These were my people. I had grown up, made friends, got married, raised my kids, served, and worked with people in evangelical circles since I was a teenager. And while the rebel part of me was thinking, *Who wants to be part of your judgy, closed-minded club anyway!* I couldn't help but feel like the vulnerable outsider, no longer welcomed by the in crowd.

Painful as Emma's words were, it also struck me that the sting I felt was just a ricochet wound compared to what Abby undoubtedly would have felt in this conversation. Maybe she'd already had ones like it and that's why she no longer wanted to come to church.

I pictured her as a toddler, the day we had a dedication ceremony for her at the church we attended then. She was curious, bright-eyed, not at all scared to be in front of all those people, the center of attention. She beamed at everyone as our pastor held her in his arms and asked the congregation to join him in praying over her life, her future. Every face in the crowd reflected back belonging, affirmation, love. A collective show of support that said, "We're here for you."

That same little girl grew up going to church with us every Sunday, playing with the kids in her Sunday school classes and midweek clubs. And that same girl, as she began to understand and come to terms with her "different" sexual orientation, began to feel unwelcome in the very circles that had embraced and loved her as a child.

I had heard similar stories from Abby's friends and others who had grown up in conservative evangelical backgrounds. Since coming out, their families wanted nothing to do with them; none of their church friends reached out to them anymore; or worse, their own parents asked them to leave home. I even heard from pastors afraid of being "let go" by their church boards if they publicly supported their gay child's decision to come out.

This wasn't a new thing. I recalled media images from the not-too-distant past of Christians carrying protest signs with slogans like "God Hates Fags" or "Homosexuals Are Possessed by Demons." I'd never once imagined, until my own daughter came out, what it must have felt like to see those signs and the people waving them through the eyes of a Christian young person struggling to understand their sexual orientation. How confusing and painful to read in those hateful words and angry faces the unmistakable message "You don't belong with us."

For Abby and other kids raised like her, church and family were very much intertwined; it would be difficult separating one from the other. To be rejected by one would feel like rejection from both. At home and at church, either directly or indirectly, Abby heard from the people she loved and looked up to most that to be gay was wrong, sinful, and against what God intended for her life. The damage that must have caused—to my child and how many others?—was too painful to try to fathom.

In my office, phone still warm on my desk, I cried out to God, the universe, and humanity with a sadness I could hardly find words for. *What have we done?* In the name of defending our beliefs, our biases, our interpretation of a handful of Bible verses, we have *uninvited* our daughters and sons from the very communities that exist to love them unconditionally. We, the body of Christ, have said, "You're not welcome here." Some of us with big, bold hateful signs; some of us with a silent cold shoulder.

How many young people had we turned away? For how many decades? Rejected by their families, called an abomination by their church, shunned by friends. All those lives filled with longing and loneliness, broken hearts.

I sobbed until my eyes burned and my shoulders ached.

Months after my phone call with Emma, still feeling the sting of her "uninvitation," I had also gained some perspective. I wish I could say it was the only time something like that happened, but it wasn't, and there will be others. I've come to understand that being excluded from some circles is the cost of sharing my story, and compared to many others, it's a small one. I joked with a friend of mine who's gay and also a Christian that I would gladly "take another one for the team" if I thought it would do any good toward bridging the chasm between these two communities we both love.

Crossing that bridge, I'm learning, starts with hard conversations like the one I had with Emma that day. We were both stammering and struggling in our own way, afraid to speak of the elephant in the room, careful not to hurt the other's feelings or challenge the other's point of view. I wish we could have another chat—maybe over coffee, with our guards down, our hearts open. I would ask Emma what she would do if her teenage daughter told her she was gay. If she saw with her own eyes that this beautiful child she had birthed was different in this way and didn't choose to be. Would she tell her daughter that this identity forming inside of her was evil, hateful to God? Would she try to convince her that she needed to change? Would she uninvite her from the family table?

I'd also want to know what the real motivation was behind Emma asking me not to come to her church and sing. What about my beliefs threatened their *unity*—a word she kept referring to? If I had to guess, I'd say the real motivation was fear.

I've seen fear tighten our circles according to our differences—be they skin color or how we interpret the Bible. Fear had been shadowing me since Abby first told me she was gay. Letting that uncomfortable truth into my heart was scary: it meant letting go of certainties about the future, about my faith, about what I had wrongly assumed about gay people. It meant asking questions and facing my own biases and ignorance. Not for the faint of heart or faith.

I'm beginning to resign myself to the fact that some people won't ever make room at God's table for people like Abby. Even harder for me to accept is that I have to make room for *them*. Tempted as I am to write off my conservative evangelical friends, the truth is, most of them are kind-hearted people who would never intentionally hurt anyone, even if their beliefs and practices inadvertently do just that. Allowing for differences on either side of the divisions between us, especially when they hit us close to home, when we have "skin in the game," is one of the hardest—and greatest—things love asks of us.

11

love and the last word

MAKING ROOM FOR AN EXPANDING FAITH

*t*here wasn't one specific *aha!* moment when I felt I had finally made sufficient room in my faith to fully accept and embrace Abby as gay. God knows the doubt and despair followed me for years, overshadowing periods of hope with more questions, new fears. It was only gradually that a sense of peace began to make its way into my heart, like tiny tributaries emptying into a sea. These moments of insight and revelation expanded my heart to make room for a deeper, broader understanding of God, the Bible, and my daughter.

If you had asked me what I believed about gay people before Abby came out, I would have given you an answer that aligned with my faith background, confidently quoting chapter and verse. I believed homosexuality was a sin—in the same way I thought adultery or stealing or lying was a sin. For the most part, that settled it for me. I had compassion for and a limited understanding of the people who suffered from this "condition," but in the end, who was I to disagree with the Bible?

Once Abby came out, it didn't take long for this simplistic view to become complicated. Coming of age in conservative evangelical culture, I had heard plenty about sin—usually as a list of nos and how to avoid them. As an adult, I came to understand sin as behavior that either hurt another or hurt the doer in some way. Even polished up, disguised, and given a fancy name, sin eventually revealed itself in bad fruit: emotional or physical pain, broken relationships, depression, bitterness—the list went on. Sin had its wages.

When trying to understand Abby's same-sex attraction within this framework, I found it confusing that the Bible called it "sin." She wasn't harming herself or anyone else as far as I could tell; she was a normal teenager in every way except she liked girls instead of boys. If pressed, I wondered if Abby could even pinpoint the moment when she first felt attracted to a girl, and if so, was that when her behavior was considered a sin according to the Bible? Or was it when she acted on that attraction in some way? I found the question perplexing.

When she first told me she was gay, I would ask Abby how she really *knew*. I even questioned her about a couple of boys she liked before coming out; it didn't make sense to me. Part of me was hoping to prove she was mistaken or confused about it, and if so, I thought I could help set her straight (no pun intended). The usual awkwardness you might imagine with those kinds of conversations ensued.

"All of my friends had boyfriends, so I just kinda thought that's what I was supposed to do," was her answer.

"Well, did you think those boys were cute?"

"Totally."

"I mean, were you attracted to them?"

"I thought I was . . . until . . ."

"Until what?"

"Until it got to a certain point. You know, like, everything would be going great, we'd be hanging out or doing something with a bunch of people and I'd feel kinda normal. I'd think, 'I can do this. I can be with a boy.'"

"So what happened to change that?"

"It was always the same thing. When we were alone and I would start to get a different vibe from them . . ."

I looked at her, waiting for her to continue. I knew this was uncomfortable, but I wanted to know how this had played out. I also wanted to know if any of these boys had been jerks and pushed her too far and if that had contributed to her thinking she was gay. I was reaching.

"As soon as a boy moved in close, like to kiss me? I felt like I was gonna throw up."

The girl was nothing if not honest. I laughed gently and said, "Honey, that's normal. I used to feel that way too with boys, the first few times things get physical like that are kind of scary. It's all so new."

She was shaking her head no. "But I've never felt like that with girls—" She stopped, flushing with embarrassment.

"You've already had . . . experiences with girls?"

"I've kissed them, yeah." She looked at me quickly, searching my face for a reaction. "And I for *sure* didn't get that sick feeling. It just felt . . . good."

At an emotional level, I understood what she was saying, but I didn't know how to process this information in a way that my faith could accept. If the Bible called what she was doing a sin, then I had to believe it was wrong. But I was confused about what part was inherently *wrong*—Abby's preference for someone of the same gender or just the act itself of kissing? Either way, I worried about the long-term implications for her future and what it meant for the possibility of a permanent relationship.

Abby had always had a soft heart toward God, praying about her dreams and hopes, though with the occasional drama of a teenage girl. But she also showed a depth of spiritual insight and wisdom beyond her years that was evidence, I believed, of a growing relationship with God. One I hoped would continue flourishing as she got older. Which is why my questions seemed to keep multiplying after she came out, turning into a quiet state of panic. What did this mean for her spiritual life? Her eternal soul? Could she still be a Christian? How could God, who "knit her together in my womb," have made a mistake with my child?

For the first time since I could remember, I questioned the goodness of God. It seemed God had given me an impossible, cruel choice: either accept Abby as she was or believe the Bible was wrong. And if I chose the latter, could I believe *any* of it was true? For someone who had been a Christian since thirteen and raised two kids in a family that loved Jesus, prayed together, and went to church every Sunday, this was no small blip on my faith radar. This was a direct hit to my core.

Desperate for answers and determined to seek them out, I got into the habit of dropping Abby off at school in the morning, then coming home and diving deep into research until it was time to pick her up. I wanted to reexamine what I was taught to see if it still held up under scrutiny. More information and other perspectives, I hoped, would shed light on familiar Bible passages and help me see them through fresh eyes.

I started by casting the widest net possible: I googled the World Wide Web. Not surprisingly, I discovered a whole lot had been written on the subject from points of view that spanned a wide spectrum. For the first couple of weeks, I floundered around in all of the articles, chat forums, blog posts, and commentary, reading and cross-referencing until I was bleary-eyed and confused. Some days, I felt overwhelmed with despair wading through all that material, no closer to having my questions answered than when I'd started.

For my own sanity, I stepped away from the web for a while and started reading actual books. No doubt my church friends would have questioned my salvation if they'd seen my Amazon purchase history. At my local Barnes & Noble, I could be seen lurking between the biblical reference and human sexuality sections, camped out on the floor in the middle of a circle of open books. Whole days passed like this—trying to absorb and process loads of information, viewpoints, analyses. I'd lose track of time, then race home in a distracted fog to throw together dinner for my family.

I decided to narrow my focus to language. As a college English major and lover of words in general, I wanted to learn what the original writers of the Bible meant by *homosexuality* and whether anything had changed in translation. A lot was hinging on this word in my own faith journey; it seemed impossible to move forward without a better understanding of it. I'm not a Bible scholar by a long shot, but it didn't take a degree to search out the findings of people who were, and what I discovered couldn't have surprised me more.

For starters, I learned that the word *homosexuality* didn't exist in any Bible translations until the mid-1900s. Once it was adopted and widely used, it brought with it a contemporary meaning that wasn't in the original language of biblical writers, which led me to wonder, What words were translators using in its place before the 1950s? A quick search yielded some lovely results such as *sodomite*, *bugger*, and *abusers of themselves with mankind*—words that clearly implied exploitation and even violence. It seemed misleading to use *homosexual* in place of those kinds of words. Obviously, like most heterosexuals I knew, most gay people weren't violent or harmful.

So while I had been equating my modern concept of "gay" with what the Bible called "homosexual," there was actually no such word in Paul's day for a person who was same-sex attracted, nor was there such a word in the Old Testament. Rather than describing a person's sexual orientation, *homosexuality* in the original Greek refers to specific kinds of sexual acts—most of them involving the exploitation of others or exerting power over another for sex. For instance, in 1 Corinthians 6:9–10 and 1 Timothy 1:9–10, Paul uses two words that don't translate clearly into English in a list that includes murder, theft, and kidnapping. Most scholars agree that both of these words refer to sexually predatory behavior from older men toward younger ones, possibly even prostitution.

I had to stop and process this for a minute. The context and original language of these verses painted a scenario that couldn't have been more different from my daughter's situation. I'd been reading those Scriptures since I was a teenager and assuming they referred to all gay people. It was shocking and humbling to realize that just a little digging revealed a much more specific meaning than what the blanket translation of *homosexuality* implied.

In the only other New Testament passage referencing homosexuality (Rom 1:25–29), the apostle Paul condemns Gentiles who refuse to believe in God and who commit "unnatural" homosexual acts as part of their idolatrous behavior. This passage is the only one mentioning women, not just men, in these kinds of acts, so I was especially keen to learn its historical and cultural context. By "unnatural" (or "against nature"), many scholars suggest that Paul was referring to sexual behavior that would have been considered either excessively lustful beyond what was normal or nonprocreative, which also would have violated Jewish cultural norms.

Seeing the context in which these verses were written helped explain the disconnect I had been experiencing with the Bible since Abby came out. I kept wondering how my teenage daughter, who loved Jesus, adored puppies, and wouldn't hurt a spider could end up on a list with first-century murderers, kidnappers, and idolaters. Was that *really* how God saw her? I was her mother and had certainly seen her at her worst, but I had never witnessed anything about Abby's sexual orientation that was threatening or hurtful toward others or herself.

I could see why it was so problematic using these verses to "prove" being gay was a sin. Nowhere in my study of the passages on homosexuality did I see a reference to consensual, loving same-sex relationships. That seemed like a significant, crucial piece of the puzzle. It was apples to oranges: comparing ancient, culturally specific sexual acts to what we now understand to be a person's sexual orientation didn't make sense.

As this new insight found its way into my head and heart, I couldn't help but share it with my husband and a few trusted friends. It wasn't unusual during dinner or at one of my book club meetings for a seemingly light conversation to turn into an in-depth analysis of biblical translation or the church's stance on homosexuality through the centuries. God bless those friends who hung in there into the wee hours some nights, trying to work out what it all meant.

A difficult question kept coming up during those late-night discussions, and I decided a little visit to the science section of the bookstore might help. My research so far had shown me that the biblical references to homosexuality condemned specific acts, not a person's orientation. But what *did* account for a person being gay, if not something inherently wrong or sinful, as I'd believed for so long? Again, lots of articles and book passages later, I discovered that even the best geneticists and scientists admit there's no simple formula for why some people are same-sex attracted. Most say it's a complex mix of factors that include DNA, biology, prenatal conditions, and early childhood development.

Some studies I read suggested that being gay, which applies to anywhere from 5 to 10 percent of the population, could be considered a naturally occurring human variant, like being born left-handed or a redhead. Much of what we're finding out now about human sexuality wasn't known until recently because of the huge leaps in technology in the past few years. Maybe old Shakespeare was right: there are more things in heaven and earth than are dreamt of in our philosophy. How could first-century biblical writers possibly have known what we now know about genetics, DNA, and other factors that contribute to a person's sexual orientation?

Seeing my daughter in this broader light was like taking off a pair of dark glasses. Certain things that had been obscured so long by my fear were now becoming clear. Dating, for example. When Abby started to pursue relationships with girls, I'd been conflicted about how to respond, afraid that she was acting immorally, in opposition to what the Bible taught. With this new insight, I was still confident in advising her against promiscuity or rushing into intimacy, but I was no longer tormented by the worry that it was biblically wrong for her to be in a relationship.

And in my most hopeful moments, though it was still a little foggy, I was starting to see a future for Abby that included love, maybe even marriage. If God created her like all of us, with an inherent desire to love and be loved, and if her sexual orientation wasn't sinful or wrong, why would this same Creator-God withhold from her the right to experience the joy and deep fulfillment of companionship? I began to make room again for the hope that she could one day be married, with a family.

I knew many Christians, including some biblical scholars, would disagree. They would argue that God's perfect design for marriage is between a man and a woman, as the Genesis account of

Adam and Eve "proves." For a parent of a child who's gay, this is a difficult point to contend with: same-sex marriage doesn't appear in the creation story; therefore, the assumption is that it must be wrong. From a strictly anatomical standpoint, I understand how a male-female couple fits the ideal design for marriage and procreation. But if companionship for Abby looks different than it does in the creation account, does that mean God intended for her not to experience it at all?

When I stop and think about what ultimately defines a good marriage, I don't think anatomy, gender, or the ability to have children rank anywhere near the top. Many couples, for example, deviate from the "biblical norm" in their inability to have children. But as someone who's been married for over thirty years, I can testify to the fact that it takes a lot more than having babies and parts that fit together to make it work. (Sorry for the frankness, but can a sister get an *amen*?) Love. Commitment. Compromise. Trust. Those are the foundations Abe and I have built a life on. They require work, sacrifice, character. I had to believe Abby was just as capable of those things as we are.

A Christian friend recently challenged me on this view, arguing that we couldn't just change biblical truth about same-sex marriage to fit the shifting culture. I considered her words carefully, then asked her to imagine if her own daughter was gay and wanted to experience the kind of lifelong companionship my friend and her husband shared. Perhaps then she'd understand that nothing in my consideration of what marriage means for my daughter came from a desire to fit into a shifting pop culture but rather to understand an underlying reality.

Certainly there were rules and practices in the Bible that Christians, including my friend, no longer followed as cultural norms have evolved. Not just Old Testament Jewish laws. Most churches have changed their stance regarding key New Testament teachings also. Beliefs about women's roles in leadership and divorce have changed, for example. The practice of slavery lost support among most churches when it became illegal, even though verses like "Slaves obey your masters" were considered biblical truth for decades and responsible for the unconscionable treatment of Black people in this country.

In some cases, it seemed to me, we needed to consider whether a higher law applied, the law of love toward our fellow human beings. How could we possibly defend a "biblical truth" if it was responsible for condemning and excluding entire populations?

My research was leading me closer to something I hadn't been able to fully grasp since Abby first came out. This yearning for a deeper, spirit-level understanding started showing up in everything I did: the songs I wrote, the journal entries I scribbled, the prayers I voiced. I knew it was time to set aside the books and stop googling the internet; all of the studying in the world couldn't tell me what I needed to know now. I began repeating a simple prayer over and over: *God, please show me your heart in this.*

Drawn to the words and acts of Jesus, I read the Gospels, this time paying closer attention to the way he treated people, who he spent time with. As I did, I discovered someone compassionate for marginalized people and scornful of the religious know-it-alls whose main objective was to catch someone breaking a law. In story after story, the Jesus I saw had no investment in blaming, judging, or condemning acts that the religious leaders had a cut-and-dried answer for. Even when they baited him with Scripture, trying to trap him by quoting the law, Jesus kept pointing to the higher law of love. He seemed more concerned with the state of people's thoughts and motives than with judging their sin.

In Jesus's words and actions, I saw the heart of this God I was so desperate to understand. God's heart wanted healing and restoration. God's heart embraced the outcast, wept with the hurting, and sent away the accusers. God's heart saw beyond class distinctions and labels to the core of every human being it encountered. God's heart declared over and over that love, not the law, has the last word.

More than just a few isolated verses, I saw that love was the thread woven throughout the Old Testament in the story of God's pursuit of Israel. Love was embodied in the person of Jesus. Love was the force behind the spreading of the good news to all people, regardless of religion, ethnicity, and gender throughout the New Testament. Jesus said the whole law, all of the commandments, could be summed up in two: love God and love one another. Paul said as much in his letter to the Corinthians when he said three things remain—faith, hope, and love, and the greatest is love.

I had begun this exploration of my faith with a fierce and unshakeable love for my daughter and an almost equally fierce desire to encounter the truth of how God saw her. I was afraid those two things would be in direct opposition, that I would have to make a choice to keep one and sacrifice the other. But what I discovered was something else. The truth I encountered in Scripture didn't contradict my notion of a loving Creator-God who wanted to be in relationship with my daughter—it confirmed it.

Believing that my daughter was part of God's good creation meant believing in a God whose every thought and intention toward her was one of love. If God's love was anything like a mother's, then I understood that love wanted for Abby and others like her the abundant life Jesus talks about, a life rooted in unconditional love, a life in which she was allowed to flourish and share it, if she so chose, with someone she loved.

It was as though my faith had been afraid to trust something so fundamentally good and simple. Or perhaps my theology needed to catch up with a deeper knowing, which, like mother's intuition, had been telling me all along my child was beloved and accepted by God just as she was.

12

why i tell it

MAKING ROOM FOR UNTOLD STORIES

i quickly discovered that this new space my faith opened up was unique and a little disorienting at first. I didn't know many people from evangelical backgrounds like mine who were accepting and affirming of the LGBTQ community. The books I was reading and people I was following online suggested that space was expanding, but straddling both worlds could be a tricky balancing act. I found myself wanting to bring together the two parts of myself into a more integrated whole. I just wasn't sure how to do it yet.

Not long ago I performed a house concert at my friend Brian's loft in Midtown Atlanta. The audience was mixed: some were Christian, most were LGBTQ, all were there for the music and the company. The house show venue was a familiar one for me; I'd done quite a few in recent years and loved sharing my songs and the stories behind them in these cozy home settings. This particular evening was the first time I would speak at length about my daughter coming out. Brian, the host, was a long-time friend who had become a trusted confidant and sounding board since Abby first came out to me. He knew my story and invited me to come and share it, along with my music, with his community.

Before going up to sing, I looked around the room. I sensed there were lots of stories in that room about the intersection of sexuality, faith, and family. Surely mine was the least dramatic. I had a moment of panic, wondering why in the world these people would want to spend an evening here, listening to one mom's story about her daughter coming out. But they listened so attentively, so graciously, it felt like a communal hug. I feared some of them wouldn't be fans of "Christian" anything, but their kindness and warmth made room for me in a way that was disarming and unexpectedly sweet.

After the concert, while I sipped wine and munched on appetizers with guests, I listened to their stories about coming out or why they hadn't yet, especially those with faith backgrounds. I heard the repeated themes of rejection, an ache to be seen and understood, a need to belong. I was moved by their honesty, and for the thousandth time, I wished with all of my heart it didn't have to be that way.

At one point, a woman sought me out in the crowd, glass of wine in hand, a skeptical look in her eye. Skipping the pleasantries, she said, "So you're a Christian, right?"

"Right."

"I'm not, but from what I understand, the Bible condemns homosexuality, doesn't it?"

Yikes, she wasn't mincing words. I tried to quickly gather my thoughts to form a complete answer. "Certain verses have been interpreted that way, historically, by most denominations, so—."

"And you *used* to believe that way, right?" she interrupted impatiently, not interested in the finer points of scriptural interpretation.

"I did, yes . . ."

"So what happened? Did you just suddenly decide to change your mind because your daughter was gay?" She fixed me with an intense, curious stare.

It was a fair question. I held her eye contact, trying to discern if she wanted to corner me and yell, "Impostor!" or if she really wanted to know how I'd made the leap in my thinking.

The truth is, I had been waiting for an airtight answer for such a time as this, a perfect thirty-second cocktail party or elevator pitch that summed up years of wrestling, researching, praying, and living with the question of how to reconcile my faith with the fact that my daughter was gay, but the truth was messy, complicated.

I answered honestly, however leaky it sounded.

"It wasn't all of a sudden, but yes, I changed my mind about what I believe. I came to understand that it's a lot more complex than what I'd assumed and been taught, and I wrestled with that for a long time. In the end, it wasn't a specific argument that changed my mind; it came down to love. I believe God created my daughter exactly as she is and loves her exactly as she is."

The woman kept her eyes locked on mine, analyzing what I'd said as she gulped down the rest of her wine. I was fully expecting her to shred my logic to pieces, but she surprised me.

"I'm glad to hear that. Gives me hope for my mom. I'm not gay, but my sister is, and my mom's a devout Catholic. She can't accept it. Maybe one day she'll change her mind too."

And then she added in that no-nonsense way I was starting to like, "Do you have all of this on your website somewhere?" She gestured with a hand, as though encircling our conversation.

I started to tell her where she could find my music, but she interrupted me again: "No, no. Your music's great, but what people really need to hear is this story."

———

The truth is, it took me years to talk about Abby being gay to anyone other than my close circle of friends. I was deeply conflicted: about my own biases and opinions, about what my evangelical upbringing had taught me, and on a very personal level, about the loss of dreams I had for the future—Abby's *and* mine. Plus, as a Christian artist and speaker, I knew it wasn't something I could openly talk about in most of the places that hired me to sing or speak.

Even if I did decide to "go public" about it, just dumping it out there without any context seemed like a colossal overshare. But my daughter had always been open about being out, and since some of our friends and contacts overlapped, not saying anything started to feel like carrying around a weighty secret. Yes, Abby's coming out was technically her story, but the more I said nothing, the more I felt I was leaving my heart and these growing truths out of all of it.

I felt compelled to say something but still waited. And as it happened, history gave me an opening. In June of 2015, just a few years after Abby came out to us, the Supreme Court made its decision to legalize gay marriage. I made my decision to "come out" publicly in a blog post about having a gay daughter. Partly, I was nudged to act at that time by the feeding frenzy of opinions online about the Supreme Court's ruling. Both sides—for and against—were out in full force, and the comments on Facebook and Twitter from a lot of Christians turned my stomach. Much of it was misinformed and ignorant. Some of it was downright hateful.

I felt it was time to say something.

After a weekend of writing, rewriting, and sobbing and trying to get the blog post right, I read it to Abby and her friend (also gay and from a Christian family), trying to get it to sound close to what my heart was saying. I posted it to my website, then shared it to my Facebook and Twitter pages. The title summed up what I hoped would come through in my writing: "What I Learned about Love When My Daughter Came Out." I wrote about how a seismic shift had occurred in my thinking when Abby came out and that over time, I had moved from ignorance and fear about what it meant for her to be gay to acceptance and love, with no strings attached.

The article received a flood of shares and likes across several platforms, including *Huffington Post's* religion section. That in turn opened up a floodgate of messages, comments, emails, and texts that revealed a world I hardly knew existed. Yes, there were plenty of opposing views from Christians pointing out the error of my thinking, quoting verses on homosexuality, or citing stories of gay people who'd "repented and turned back to God" and were now living heterosexual, happy lives. But most of the responses I received were from people sharing their own stories of coming out or about a family member who was LGBTQ.

Overnight, my world and my heart felt enlarged with these messages. Of course there were other Christian families like ours navigating the unfamiliar waters of having a gay child; I had just been oblivious to them, too caught up in my own struggle. Having been quiet for as long as I was about it, I think I'd convinced myself that ours was an isolated experience.

Some of the messages and comments I received were from young gay women whose own parents hadn't arrived at the same place of acceptance as I had. Those broke my heart more than any of the others. One woman wrote, "I'm sure you can imagine how my 'perfect church parents' took the news when I came out to them all those years ago. I was not 'disowned,' but . . . as long as it isn't mentioned, then they can 'love me.' Nothing is ever said, but I have found that silence can be the most painful form of communication there is."

Other messages and comments came from Christian moms in the same situation as me. It shouldn't have been such a revelation, I know, but it was comforting to know I wasn't alone. Their notes were hands reaching out across the internet, grabbing mine and squeezing them in solidarity.

I recalled how frightened I'd been right after Abby came out when I read one mother's message, telling me she had just googled "My daughter is gay, now what do I do?" and my blog post came up. "It was my story," she wrote. "There are times I feel I can hardly breathe. I too grew up with the mentality that all gays are hated by God, but then your own child comes out and suddenly you realize there has to be more . . . God doesn't make mistakes."

Another mom wrote to me saying she had a son who was gay and that she mourned some of the same losses I had, while almost no one in her circle of Christian friends understood their family's journey. She ended by saying, "I wish I had known there was another mom sitting beside me in the pews who understood my heart."

Some notes were from veteran moms who'd been on the field long before I got there and had precious, hard-won wisdom to share. They helped shed light on the possibility of a future for Abby and for our whole family. These moms challenged me, too, to stretch my heart wider and bigger.

> When my daughter came out to us . . . 18 years ago . . . I was sad for her, not because she was gay, but for all that I believed she would not have: a spouse and family. Last September, she married her partner of 15 years. They have a beautiful daughter (my daughter's biological child). They have been a family for years, and the legalization of that right has brought joy beyond measure. We are Christians. I don't see this this as incompatible. I never have. I cried after learning of the Supreme Court

ruling. Now my family can be legally protected wherever they go. As a parent, that is a huge relief.

One mom shared my blog post, along with these words to her friends and family:

This is everything I've ever tried to put into words about my son but couldn't. These are the words I wanted to say during your debates with me. These are the words I wanted to say when you told me "in love" my son was sinning. These are the words I wanted to say when you told me you'd pray for my son to change. These are the words I wanted to say when you told me a Christian mother can't possibly be an ally for her gay son. These are the words I wanted to say when you told me that celebrating who my son is would make him "gayer." These are the words I wanted to say when you tried to convince me something was wrong with my child that needed to be fixed. These are the words I wanted to say when I tried to explain unconditional love to you, as you put conditions on your love for me, for my son and our family.

Pastors and church leaders mentoring kids who had come out sent private messages, thanking me for telling our story, admitting they weren't able to speak of it publicly and felt isolated. There are real-world consequences for Christians in the public eye who land on the "wrong" side of this topic. Author Jen Hatmaker and musician Vicky Beeching, along with many others, paid a high price for speaking out on behalf of the LGBTQ community. Their CDs and books were stripped from Christian retailers' shelves and websites, and the bulk of their speaking and singing dates for evangelical crowds quickly dried up.

The fact that my blog post generated so much conversation proved the point of my frank friend from the house concert—this was a story people need to hear. Since writing it, whenever I sing or speak somewhere, it's inevitable that someone will approach me quietly afterward, tell me they read my blog post about Abby, and then share their own story about someone in their family who's gay.

Those conversations aren't happening out loud in the churches I visit—not yet, anyway—but they're being whispered by people who are either hurting, confused, or just feeling isolated. Whether or not we choose to acknowledge them, there are people sitting next to us in the pews, across from us at Bible study, beside us in choir, whose lives are being touched by this topic, either directly or indirectly. So many remain silent because they think they're the only ones or because they're afraid of speaking out against what their church teaches.

And yes, fear also played a part in my waiting to come out publicly in support of my daughter. I was afraid of what people would think of me—that I'd be seen as an extremist, a troublemaker. I was afraid of losing gigs in my line of work. I was afraid of being called out on my beliefs and seen as theologically weak or compromised. I was afraid I'd be perceived as too conservative for progressive Christians already advocating for the LGBTQ community and too liberal for evangelicals who held more traditional views of gender roles and marriage.

But I'm learning how important it is to make room for the stories of people whose experiences are different from mine, especially if they've been silenced, made to feel ashamed, or told their stories didn't matter.

I'm learning to make room for the kind of radical grace Jesus practiced: healing, restoring, and welcoming those marginalized by the religious majority.

I'm learning to make room for faith in a God who is more about letting people in than keeping them out.

This is only one small story. My heart has much more stretching and growing to do, guided by the great and big heart of God. But I trust life will continue to bring people and opportunities my way that will expand and push at the boundaries I put on love.

And if I tell this one small story about a girl God and I are crazy about, who happens to be gay, maybe someone hearing it will think differently about their son or niece or that neighbor whose gender or sexual identity is a mystery. Maybe they'll look them in the eye and listen when they talk about what it's like to be them.

And ultimately, if our LGBTQ kids and neighbors and coworkers feel less alone in the world because we've made room for them—in our churches, in our hearts, in our vision for the future—and they feel seen and heard and welcomed, then it's worth whatever it costs any of us to tell our one small story.

afterword

MAKING ROOM FOR
A REIMAGINED FUTURE

$t$he doorbell rang, and I headed toward the entryway, tossing aside the dish towel I'd just used to pull a tray of stuffed mushrooms out of the oven. That would be Abby, and I couldn't wait to give her a squeeze. Between my Christmas concerts and her busy schedule, it had been weeks since I'd seen her—too long, as far as I was concerned. I've always missed my kids as soon as they walk out my front door. It was Christmas Eve, and I was ready to fill my heart and home with their laughter and conversations.

I opened the door wide and Abby stood on the front porch, her arms filled with a pile of presents so high I couldn't see her face, just her black suede hat peeking over the top. It was one of those wide-brimmed bohemian styles, her latest trademark look. She's one of those rare people who can pull off wearing a hat like that to the grocery store, a family Christmas dinner, or onstage—and look natural.

Next to her stood Kelsie, the tall, blonde, fresh-faced beauty she'd been dating for over two years. A down-to-earth and kind soul—I adored her. They both looked festive, happy to be visiting the folks for the holidays.

Before I could get a word out, a whirling ball of fur darted at me from between the girls, attempting to jump up and lick my face in a happy, wet greeting.

"Down, River!" they said in unison, to no avail. River, their five-month-old golden retriever puppy, was beside herself with excitement. I laughed and knelt down to give her some love.

"Merry Christmas, Mom!" Abby said, poking her head around the pile of presents.

"Hello, hello! Merry Christmas to *you*!" I said, reaching around the gifts to kiss her cheek.

A bittersweet ache overcame me as I looked at her and, in that one glance, saw every age she'd ever been. Hadn't I *just* taken this six-year-old girl to Toys"R"Us, where she'd lost her Hello Kitty wallet and sobbed inconsolably in my arms? The years had passed at light speed. What else could account for this grown-up standing on my front porch? Put-together, self-assured, confident. She looked like a bona fide adult, bearing Christmas gifts she'd bought with her own money and wrapped at her own apartment.

Merciful Lord, my girl had become a woman.

I struggled past the sudden urge to weep and found my voice. "And Merry Christmas to you, Kelsie! I'm so glad you could be with us!"

Kelsie flashed me a big smile, warm and genuine. "Me too!"

I waved them inside, toward the twinkling Christmas tree, where they unloaded their gifts gingerly—there were a *lot* of them. I realized Kelsie must have brought presents for the family and immediately wished there was more than just a candle for her under the tree. Next year I would definitely do better.

"Are you hungry?"

The girls nodded in unison and headed toward the kitchen, where the rest of the family fussed over River and hovered near the appetizers.

I surveyed the group from across the room: my oldest (Zach) and his girlfriend; my sister from Nashville, here to spend Christmas with us, a rare treat; and my mom and Abe's mom, both widows, who were hardly ever with us at the same time. This would be our first Christmas with everyone together in the new house, the one we'd finally purchased after several years of renting and recovering from the housing market crash. The joy was almost too much to take. I was already choking back tears for the second time, and the evening had just started.

More than just nostalgia, I could feel something stirring way back in my memory. A kind of déjà vu, a dream I thought I'd said goodbye to all those years ago sitting in my empty garage looking up at a wedding dress box in the rafters. Mourning the loss of a home, a future. Looking around me, I saw my home now filled with the ones I loved most and the people *they* loved. Wasn't that the very vision I'd hoped for? Surreal. Life had come full circle.

River interrupted my nostalgic reverie, dropping a squeaky toy at my feet. She wanted to play tug-of-war, and I couldn't resist her because I couldn't say no to anything this puppy wanted. To understand how hard I fell for her, you need to know that I'm not a dog person. I don't dislike dogs; it just takes me a long time to get comfortable around them. The shedding, the odor, the slobber. It's a lot.

My daughter fell from a different tree when it comes to dogs—her father's; people call them both dog whisperers. Since she was little, Abby has known she would one day have a dog, a golden retriever, to be exact, of her own. After high school, she traveled for a few years playing music and doing freelance video work, and she didn't feel settled enough to make the commitment. Or, rather, we had to *convince* her she wasn't settled enough.

Apparently, life with Kelsie had changed all that because not only had they decided to get an apartment together; they had also opted to get a pup. One visit was all it took for me to fall in love with River. Her sweet puppy breath, her velvety soft paws, her awkward little gallop—I was completely smitten. I went a little crazy: I bought toys, a doggie faux-fur bed, and even considered letting her up on my nearly new couch, prompting my husband to ask, "Who *are* you?"

I saw his point. I vetoed the couch idea, but we both knew that little golden pup had cracked something open in me.

Maybe it sounds silly, but seeing my daughter with River awakened a long-buried hope hard to articulate since Abby came out. It was a joy so pure for *her* joy, my daughter's, at raising this little pup with the person she loved. I watched as she nurtured River, loving and tender, learning to put her own needs aside. I realized that my girl had all the makings of a good mama. I saw a glimpse, a prelude, of what a real family could be like for Abby, for all of us.

On Facebook, some of my friends have started posting pictures of their grandbabies with captions about how absolutely delighted they are by these little additions to the family. I've hardly allowed myself to imagine what that could be like with a gay daughter. It seemed too far-fetched, impossible. Even though logic told me there were options for same-sex couples who wanted to have children, my heart had been reluctant to believe it could ever be a reality for Abby.

Seeing Abby in a relationship that had long-term, marriage potential, I wanted to hope again that our family would grow. I wanted to hope that she'd be able to experience the wonder of all wonders: being a mother. And I desperately wanted to believe that I would get to share that with her. I had not allowed myself that kind of hope for a long, long time.

One of my daughter's gifts is the ability to capture moments beautifully on camera. A favorite picture of mine was a close-up of the girls' hands and River's paw, which Abby had framed for me with the simple caption "This is us. #fambly." I saw a message in that picture: Abby's family portraits, whatever they looked like in the years to come, would be different from what I imagined for her when she was a little girl. A reminder that making room for a different vision of Abby's future might turn out to be okay after all. Maybe even surprisingly wonderful.

After dinner, we lingered around the table and took turns sharing what we were most thankful for that year—a tradition we'd started years ago and that my kids didn't mind revisiting, in spite of the fact that their dad and I almost always ended up crying at some point during the share-fest. There was much to be thankful for this year and much to look forward to in each of my children's futures.

I looked over at my son, now a man, and the beautiful brown-eyed girl he had his arm around. They'd been together for a couple of years, were crazy in love, and I had to wonder, Would they get married one day soon and have kids who would play in our backyard? Would they have her olive complexion, his blue eyes?

I glanced at Abby, and she caught my eye and smiled. She looked at Kelsie and River sideways and back at me again with raised eyebrows, as if to say, "What do you think of my little family?" I gave her a slow nod and hoped she could feel my joy at seeing her so happy.

There was a glow in the room that night, like grace, hovering over and around and between us. Grace softening the edges of our pain, healing our wounds, stirring our hope. It was one of those rare and holy times when a sense of peace and acceptance of things as they were flooded through me. The painful memories of the past and anxious what-ifs of tomorrow hung suspended in time as I felt only gratitude. For another year of life, for each other, for God and the goodness we'd experienced through the years.

It felt transcendent, magical.

And perhaps more profound to me in that moment, it felt perfectly ordinary.

acknowledgments

*i*t's been ten years since our daughter came out to us and five since I started writing this book. Along the way, there have been so many friends, mentors, readers, and encouragers who helped make its publication a reality, it feels nearly impossible to thank them all. Though I will inevitably leave some out, I want to express my gratitude to the people who played particularly meaningful roles in the telling of this story.

My editors at Broadleaf Books lovingly and professionally chiseled away at bulkier versions of this book, shaping and polishing it to bring the message into sharper focus. I'm grateful for their expertise and kindness.

My rock star agent, Rachelle Gardner, took a chance on an unpublished author and championed a story we knew would be tricky to navigate through the publishing process. Her belief in this book, and in me as a writer, steadied me throughout the entire daunting process. I'm honored to call her my agent and my friend.

When I had the first draft written and no idea what to do with it, Doug and Sheryl Griffin reentered my life, sharing their own story with me and offering their generous support. Their encouragement was the nudge I needed to take the next steps, for which I'll be forever grateful.

Throughout the writing process, I sent various versions of the manuscript to friends, asking for their feedback. Melissa Campbell Goodson, Judy Mikalonis, Jeff McIntosh, and Christy Tyler cheered me on with their timely and helpful comments and responses. Lori Sabin and Mandi Higgins went above and beyond, not only reading early drafts, but also engaging with me in millions of texts, phone calls, and conversations about this book. I'm indebted to both of them.

My early mentors in all things LGBTQ, Laura Koepnick and Brian Nietzel, graciously let me ask all sorts of unfounded, awkward questions and never once judged me for it. Their friendship was—and still is—a priceless gift.

Several trailblazers showed me what it looked like to love their LGBTQ children fiercely and wrestle with their faith unashamedly in the public square: Sara Cunningham of Free Mom Hugs, Greg and Lynn McDonald of Embracing the Journey, Liz Dyer of the Serendipity for Moms Facebook group, and all of the brave mama bears. Their examples fueled my courage to share this story.

Countless LGBTQ people, parents, and other allies have reached out to me with their heartbreaking stories, including many who were rejected by their families, churches, and friends. Their stories are a daily reminder to me of the need for more compassionate, informed conversations about this topic.

Finally, my family: Abe let me disappear for a while to write this book and has been my steadfast companion on this "making room" journey from the start. Zachary modeled unconditional acceptance and love early on in the process. And Abby bravely allowed me to tell my side of a story that is multidimensional, still unfolding—and mostly hers. She fiercely and tenderly continues to teach me how to make room for more understanding and love.